Advance Praise for *The Layoff Cooties*

Laura Krauss bares it all. Her heart, her sadness, her anger, and her rebirth after job loss. This book is a must read for anyone who has ever been laid off. It is a rising-from-the-ashes story for the modern day professional, and with witty tales, sage advice, and the wisdom that comes from real experience, you will ride the roller coaster of emotions, all while saying, "this has been me."

~ Robynn Storey, CEO,
Storeyline Resumes and Author of *Career Confidence: No-BS Stories and Strategies for Finding Your Power*

This is a powerful story, and my heart goes out to Laura Krauss. She went through a lot. In the span of 4 minutes, she lost a job she loved along with many friendships. Losing a job is like losing a piece of yourself. It's tough to recover. Laura shows us that you can get back up after loss. Inside, you will witness her courage and testimony of how one can experience loss unexpectedly and still pick up the pieces to create the next adventure in your career.

~ Deborah Brown-Volkman,
Chief Career Officer and Career Goals Guru

Powerful. Vulnerable. Courageous. Laura's layoff story normalizes the all too familiar, but not spoken about, effects of corporate layoffs. This is a must read!

~ Suzanne Roske,
Vamonos Executive Coaching, Author of
I'm Supposed To Be Doing This: An Adult Gap Year

We read about the giant faceless numbers all the time and most have become numb to the collateral damage that layoffs cause. Laura has written a compelling and touching story of her own gut-wrenching journey through her layoff and a definitive field guide to help others navigate the roller coaster of emotions they will need to navigate in their layoff journey. Laura has done a beautiful job humanizing her experience so that others can learn and grow. Exceptional read.

~ Scott MacGregor, Founder and CEO of SomethingNew LLC , Founder of The Outlier Project , Publisher and Editor-In-Chief of Outlier Magazine

---

Laura's generous story is laid here, raw and vulnerable. It will help so many that have been, may be, or will be laid off. It will help those supporting people affected by layoffs. Laura's book will have you reexamining your priorities and seeing your experiences in a new light. It will validate you and leave you with hope. That there is truly no end, rather a new beginning. As humans, we seek validation of our feelings. Laura has gifted so much of that here. Gift yourself this book.

~ Beth Stowell Reed, Lover of Stories and Human Being

If you've been laid off, you'll want to read "The Layoff Cooties-It's Them, Not You" now! If your friends have been laid off, you'll need "The Layoff Cooties-It's Them, Not You" to empathize with your friends. Either way, Laura Krauss pulls back the curtain on what happens and how it makes you feel.

~ Dr. John Page, Founder, Reacher Development LLC, former pastor

"*The Layoff Cooties—It's Them, Not You*" is a powerful read that brilliantly captures the challenges women face as they rise in sales, especially when navigating workplace politics. Laura's storytelling vividly portrays the deep emotional impact of losing work relationships due to corporate decisions, and the personal trauma of being laid off. She provides a compassionate space for readers to grieve and reflect, making this book a valuable resource for anyone grappling with job loss.

~ Heather Bell, Founder of Top Software Sales Performer Program for Women

---

"*The Layoff Cooties*" is such a great read. Laura Krauss takes you through the raw emotions of a layoff—from the backstory, the event and the what's next. This powerful recount of being an assertive servant leader and the silence of former co-workers is a very relatable reality that resonates in corporate America. This book guides the newly unemployed on how to process emotions and change a career narrative one step at a time. Her story is ultimately about the resilience of a leader who reframes how she brings her leadership to a new audience and shows up every day in ways that she didn't imagine.

~ Sarah Manley, MA, Global Talent Marketing Executive

Through her candid storytelling, Laura captures the heartache and the profound loss that comes with being let go from a job. Her honest reflections and practical advice for navigating this challenging experience make this book a must read for anyone facing similar circumstances. I know, I went through it myself as well. The book brought it all back to the forefront for me. It's a powerful reminder that even in our darkest moments, there is a path forward. A beautifully written journey of resilience and hope.

~ Dennis Geelen,
Author of *The Accidental Solopreneur:
From burn-out to freedom. A parable.*

Moving and sobering, encouraging and challenging, Laura Krauss' relatable story will resonate with anyone in today's workforce—employees and employers alike—whose orbits include the ever-present threat of layoff. She pulls back the curtain on this very tumultuous time in her life, authentically sharing not only the rawness of her surprise and anger, but also revealing her path toward healing. "The Layoff Cooties-It's Them, Not You" is not just about suffering a termination; it is about how to rise from the ashes of any form of rejection. Laura's story serves as a powerful reminder that our true identity cannot be found in a career or salary, in recognition or relationships, but only in the One who always loves us unconditionally.

~ Diane Higginbothem,
Retired Colonel USAF, Christ-follower, and friend

This is the book I wish I had when I lost my job in 2012, while on track to finish the year 162% of my goal! Laura's bravery to share so vulnerably is refreshing, approachable and so needed. Her storytelling drew me in and left me wanting more, so much so I couldn't put the book down.

~ Erin Harrigan, Erin Harrigan Coaching

Thanks to Laura Krauss for writing a guide that is so needed in the market today. This book offers a profound, definitive guide on how to be true to your identity after a difficult layoff.

~ Heidi Solomon-Orlick, Founder and CEO, GirlzWhoSell and Author of *Heels to Deals: How Women are Dominating in Business-to-Business Sales*

This book comes at a time when we're experiencing layoffs like never before! Laura writes with such candor and honesty that I believe every reader needs to hear. She weaves us through the story of her layoff and how it impacted her physically as well as emotionally. It took me back to a time when I felt so many of those things through a layoff. She leaves no stone unturned in sharing her story, but most of all she shares her tenacity and strength and why she believes her layoff led to discovering her true purpose in life.

~ Leslie Wierich, Author of *The Gifts of Grief: How Four Decades of Loss Shaped My Life*

Laura does an incredible job of putting the reader in the shoes of a highly accomplished and successful sales leader, blindsided with a termination and the emotional, professional, and personal impact that has. It shows that no one is safe, not even top performers. She highlights a common occurrence of abandonment that often occurs with trusted friends and co-workers. She gives an accurate depiction of the trauma associated with terminations that so many can relate to. Give it a read—there is something in it for everyone who has gone through a challenging termination—something both the employee and employer can learn from.

~ Dan Goodman,
Founder, Dan Goodman Employment Advisory

What I loved most about reading this book was how it allowed me to step into the author's experience—something I've never personally faced. The story deepened my empathy not just for the author, but for anyone who might go through a similar situation. Now, I feel equipped with a much clearer understanding if I experience others who are facing these challenges. A great read for anyone, really! We all know someone who has been here.

~ Renee Wright, Leadership and Life Coach

The Layoff Cooties— It's Them, Not You

From Rejection to Redirection and Finding Your Ripple Effect Again

LAURA KRAUSS

Copyright © 2024 by Laura Krauss. All rights reserved.

Published by Ripple Effect Sales Advisory LLC

No part of this publication may be reproduced or transmitted in any form or by any means, electronic, mechanical, photocopying, recording, scanning, or otherwise without the prior written permission of the Publisher. Requests to the Publisher for permission should be addressed to laura@rippleeffectsales.com.

The views expressed in this publication are those of the author. This book is a work of nonfiction. Some names and identifying details have been changed.

First Edition

Library of Congress Control Number: 2024916663

ISBN: 979-8-9909739-0-9
BUS012030 BUSINESS & ECONOMICS / Careers / Career Advancement & Professional Development

Cover Design by The Soulful Book Designer, Toni Serofin at Sanserofin Studio

*To the LinkedIn community, who became my
"work friends" after the Layoff Cooties bit me
on November 29, 2023.*

*Your supportive DMs, caring comments,
and loveable likes restored my faith in humanity.*

*You helped me to heal from immense grief
after losing my job in ways I can never repay.*

You know who you are.

THANK YOU.

———

*There once was a girl set free
To be all that she could be.
Her words showed up here,
To release all the fear.
This book is vulnerably me.*

# Contents

How to Use This Book   i

1   Paying It Forward   1

2   Playing the Game   15

3   Game Over   35

4   Shock—This Can't Be Happening   57

5   Denial—Top Performers Don't Get Laid Off   71

6   Anger—This Is Not Who I Want to Be   83

7   Bargaining—What If versus Imagine If   115

8   Depression—Been There, Done That   123

9   Testing—Does Anyone Really Know What Works?   133

10   Acceptance—The Gift I Gave Myself   151

11   From Rejection to Redirection   165

12 Finding Your Ripple Effect Again 179

Cooties Q & A 189

Acknowledgments 195

About the Author 203

 # How to Use This Book

Welcome to the book I never thought I would ever write. Yet, here we are.

I truly loved my job as regional vice president of Customer Growth sales. I was excellent at it. That's not me bragging; executive leadership, respected colleagues, implementation partners, customers I supported, young women I mentored, and sales reps I led repeatedly told me I excelled in my work. I believed it because it was true. My strong performance achieved positive results, and I did so by serving others. As women, we don't give ourselves enough credit for all our accomplishments, and I won't perpetuate that mistake by selling my success short.

To have someone else control where I worked and who I worked with shattered me to my core. Without my job, I didn't know who I was. It was part of my identity as much as my big brown eyes. Perhaps that was my fault for valuing myself too much through my work, but I don't think it's unusual for anyone trying to be the best version of themselves.

In the days and months after my unexpected layoff on November 29, 2023, I started writing on LinkedIn. Until then, I only used LinkedIn to find career information on my prospects and customers. I rarely posted content, but I desperately needed connection and poured my heart into writing daily posts. Writing on LinkedIn offered me a therapeutic release; I craved it every day.

People across industries and disciplines quickly followed me as my stories resonated with them. I found solace in reading the comments and seeing one of the six colorful emojis (blue thumbs up, green clapping celebration, purple open-palm support, red-hearted love, yellow insightful light bulb, and that turquoise funny guy smiling).

While it may sound silly, those emojis and comments on LinkedIn had a ripple effect on my soul. People cared about me again—beyond my family, who knew the pain the layoff caused me. I also knew my former colleagues could read my posts, at least those who hadn't blocked me. When one of them commented or left a reaction, I noted it, but mostly I observed how many didn't pay attention to my posts. That was just as telling, and it crushed my psyche. Writing this book, and having a public record of my layoff experience, are part of my healing process. I don't want to be forgotten. I won't be a statistic in the "Tech Layoffs of 2023" that numbered in the tens of thousands. My story matters and it needs to be told.

Not all of us will write a book.

Not all of us will express in writing what a layoff truly feels like.

Not all of us want a public record of our emotions for the world to read.

My hope in sharing my story is that you will feel seen and heard in yours.

Your story matters too.

How to Use This Book

And, perhaps something from your story piqued enough curiosity to learn more about mine, and that connects us forever. It reminds me of an old Chinese proverb: "An invisible thread connects those who are destined to meet, regardless of time, place, or circumstance. The thread may stretch or tangle, but it will never break."

While I can never know every reader's background, I'm inclined to believe that you or someone you know experienced a layoff. (Maybe you have an extra couple of bucks and a few hours to spend reading a book with a funny title).

What exactly are layoff cooties, anyway? Cooties are a childish term for an imaginary germ or disease that one catches by associating with another person who people dislike or avoid. The term rejects people socially. It intends to shun. No one wants the cooties.

Layoff cooties mean people reject someone who the company lays off. People avoid their former coworkers by insinuating that once a company lays someone off, former colleagues must stop communicating with them. Perhaps these people fear the layoff is contagious, and they will be next. Perhaps they don't know what to say, so they choose to say nothing. Maybe it's the fear cultivated by executive management to control the corporate narrative by giving directives to cut off ties with former coworkers. Regardless of the reason, people don't want to catch whatever it is that caused that former colleague to lose their job.

Nearly everyone I met while writing this book (over 400 individual layoff interviews from my first six months posting on LinkedIn) spoke of the layoff-cooties phenomenon. My unscientific experiment with a small cross section of society isn't enough to coin a newly accepted term, but it has sticking power. It's not going anywhere anytime soon!

My book, however, doesn't focus on someone else's layoff experience. It's about my life and downfall within a sales organization at a job I truly loved and thought I would hold until I reached retirement. I believed in the organization's vision. I represented my company's well-respected brand name with pride. And most importantly, I loved the people I worked with and believed they were more than colleagues. I cared for them as friends.

Most people focus on the financial aspects of job loss as being the worst part of a layoff. This is well-documented. Losing my six-figure W-2 forced my family to adjust because I was the breadwinner with the highest salary. The more devastating blow, however, was the emotional and relational part of realizing that the people I worked with, and thought were genuine friends, had no room for me in their lives anymore.

Losing those friendships is what I miss the most. No one, I believe, talks nearly enough about the emotional impact of a layoff. That's one of the reasons I wanted to share my story.

Things to know as you read this book

My greatest strength is connecting authentically with others through my vulnerability. As a twenty-five-year sales veteran, I led my sales teams with trust and empathy to create a psychologically safe work environment. Much in the same way, I want to provide a haven as you journey through my layoff experience through this book. There's power in sharing our stories, and I am honored you are reading mine.

My goals for writing this book are threefold:

1. I want to share my personal experience as a top-performing software sales leader, blindsided by a targeted and politically motivated layoff.
2. I want you to know that the raw, visceral feelings of loss are normal; I also want you to recognize there is no defined timeline for grieving.
3. I want you to realize that rejection from a layoff redirects you to your next big thing in life. You can and will work again!

Whether you are laid off (the one with the cooties), the coworker left behind from a layoff (you don't want to get the cooties), or you are a family member of someone laid off (you love the person with the cooties), my story has the power to help each infected, I mean, affected reader.

I respect the confidentiality of those who played an integral part in the pain I experienced since the fallout from that infamous day. To protect former colleagues, I changed their names. A small subset of people who read my book may know the identities of former colleagues based on the events, but it's not my intention to bring negative publicity to their lives or hurt them. Their actions (or inactions) created emotional reactions in me, a ripple effect people impose on one another playing out one day at a time. (You know…that invisible thread I was talking about earlier).

There is no need to name the company who terminated me. You will not find the name anywhere in these pages because the company didn't do any of these things to me. The colleagues working there, the ones I trusted, believed in, and supported for years, hurt me. Just know the company was a best-of-breed, global software-as-a-service (SaaS) company where I worked for almost four years. That's more than enough time to have made my mark, leaving a respectable impression and professional legacy that I am very proud of today.

Additionally, my Christian faith is found throughout these pages. I understand you have your opinions about God, and I respect the experiences governing your viewpoint. My request is that you, as the reader, respect mine in return.

I always believed in God, but it wasn't until my mid-thirties that I began a real relationship with Him. Through that very personal one-on-one relationship, I know He guides me on my path to live out my purpose. To clarify who or what I think God is, quite simply God is love. And He has given me the strength to love and share my story with the world, in hope that it will help others.

One more thing before you turn the page. Allow me to give you "the tour." The first three chapters introduce you to my world in corporate America, specifically software sales. It's where I recently spent nearly ten years of my sales career enjoying much success within the tech industry. The first fifteen years of my professional career were also in sales. I was fortunate to gain valuable experience in the hospitality, biotech/pharmaceutical, and medical publishing industries in various sales operations roles. I also tried my hand in franchise ownership, which I tell people was the best and worst experience of my life.

My reason for sharing these early career experiences is to highlight my growing love for the sales profession and how I navigated the emotional roller coaster of a twenty-five-year career. If you think about it, everyone is in sales. We're all selling some part of ourselves in the way we interact with one another, and as a result, building strong relationships

How to Use This Book

becomes paramount. Perhaps that's why losing those relationships causes trauma.

Chapters 4 through 10 highlight the seven stages of grief as it relates to healing from my layoff experience. Grief is not linear. The journey toward healing doesn't move in a straight line in any one direction. It zigs and zags, reaches up and down, and often feels like you're taking three giant steps backward to make one small step forward. That's normal.

If you've experienced a layoff, I challenge you to think about your journey as you read these chapters. Do you feel stuck in one stage more than another? Did you skip over some early stages only to find yourself right back at the beginning stages in the days, weeks, or months after your layoff? Do you hide from opening yourself up to experiencing any one of these seven stages? Don't worry; there's no right or wrong answer. But I do believe there's healing in contemplating those questions.

Grief carries many layers. What one person easily recovers from, another painfully can't get over. That's normal too. I'm a big believer in the perspective that grief isn't something you get over; it's something you get through. I don't think grief ever ends or goes away. Nor do I think it's supposed to. It's part of the complete human experience. For as many billions of people there are in the world, there are equally many billions of ways people deal with grief. Let's allow each one the grace they deserve to heal in the ways and on the timelines they deem necessary.

The final two chapters explore transitioning from the rejection my layoff brought to a new, unexpected redirection. As I planned for life after the layoff, I often pivoted in several directions. Each time, however, I came back to a personal philosophy I coined early in my sales career. My mantra was living a sales life with EASE: Everything is Attitude, Skill, and Effort. We each have a choice regarding the attitude we show up with each day, the skills we choose to learn, and the effort we put forth. No matter where you work or what you do, no one else can take those three things away from you. Think about it. It's true. The cool part is, it doesn't just work in sales. It works in life.

In the Cooties Q&A section, there are thought-provoking questions you can journal more deeply, or, at the very least, gain a different perspective to ponder. Maybe you read this book on your own or as part of a book club group. My goal is to start conversations, if they are with yourself and/or others, that healing can begin. This will look different for everyone, but the Q&A section at the end of the book is meant to evoke and elicit deeper contemplation. You'll find a QR code directing you to a form where you can share your answers with me directly. You have my commitment if you take time to answer the questions. I will read each one and communicate back with a thoughtful response. I love engaging with my community on LinkedIn as well, and you'll find my profile link in the "About the Author" section should you want to connect with me there.

I thank you for reading my story. We live in a world where time and money are precious resources. I don't take for granted your investment. If you purchased this book on Amazon, I would appreciate a review. Good, bad or indifferent, your opinion matters to me (and the world), and I'd be honored if you provided your feedback.

Sharing and recommending "The Layoff Cooties—It's Them, Not You" with friends and family who can relate to cootie infections is the perfect remedy to begin healing from a traumatizing layoff. I hope my story validates the human emotions that occur as you get through, not over, a layoff.

God bless.

1 Paying It Forward

I've been interested in sales for as long as I can remember. My mom was a small business owner on the South Shore of Long Island, New York, where I grew up. I went to work with her from a very young age and subconsciously learned the importance of building relationships with customers and knowing how to ask the right questions to help people on their buying journey. From my mom's simple, yet profound example, I learned how to deal with challenging business situations. She was my first female role model, a leader at work and in our home, and a mentor without me even realizing it until I was much older.

One day, when I was about ten years old, a little girl was shopping with her mother in my mom's gift shop, an old house adorned with home decor items and boutique style gifts sprinkled throughout the building. The house was two levels, with multiple hidden rooms throughout. While the mother shopped downstairs, the little girl went upstairs and put some items in her pockets without paying. This was before the days when video recording was commonplace everywhere in stores. The mother didn't realize what her daughter had done until they got home. She immediately drove her back to my mom's store to return them.

The Layoff Cooties – It's Them, Not You

The little girl was crying as she apologized to my mom. Without a beat, my mom crouched down at eye level and calmly asked the little girl if she learned her lesson.

Still crying, she nodded yes.

My mom gifted the small items to the little girl and said: "I'm proud of you for apologizing and doing the right thing. Keep this as a gift and reminder to 'pay it forward.' Always teach others to speak the truth."

The mother of the little girl insisted she pay for the items, but my mom would not hear of it. Lessons like this are powerful when witnessing first hand. How lucky was I to see my mom in action when I, too, was so young?

Two little girls learned a lesson that day.

Now, as a grown woman, I think of all the pay-it-forward moments that transpired in my twenty-five years in sales (and forty-five years in life). I was never a small business owner like my mom, but I worked in corporate America for most of my professional career. It gave me plenty of chances to pay it forward and speak the truth when bad behavior reared its ugly head. (More on that soon).

I'm going to give you my professional background because I think it's important to highlight my sales journey before I began working at the company that laid me off. My career wasn't something that only provided a paycheck every two weeks. I valued myself by my work and the way I showed up every single day for whichever employer I represented. That's not to say I didn't find value in my personal life as a daughter, sister, wife, and mother, but the responsibility I had in each of my sales roles was an opportunity to showcase my strong business acumen, integrity in relationship building, and leadership skills.

By the time I reached my early thirties, I had built a strong resume and successful career in sales operations at well-known hospitality and pharmaceutical companies. I held in-house roles at corporate headquarters, working behind the scenes to support sales organizations as they scaled and grew. I loved my sales-operations-based teams and the accomplishments we achieved, but I always felt something greater called my name.

I walked away from that career track in 2007 to try my hand in franchise ownership, hoping to live the entrepreneurial dream (a.k.a. nightmare) of owning a business. That chapter of my life is a book within itself so here's the shortened version: With hundreds of thousands of dollars invested and a bankruptcy that almost killed me (literally and figuratively), I found myself back in corporate America again after a few years of franchise ownership. By then, it was 2011, so I returned to sales operations roles for a few more years.

In 2015, I accepted a leadership role—my dream job at the time—as a Sales Operations manager at an allergy/pharmaceutical company. One of my initial projects was leading the evaluation for a new travel and expense management system to replace an outdated manual one. Employees were mailing in paper receipts and not getting reimbursed for sixty to ninety days later. It was a huge problem, not only for the growing sales organization, but also for the folks in the back-end finance office responsible for reimbursing employees in a timely fashion. I led the evaluation of vendors and eventually chose SAP Concur as our trusted partner to digitize and automate an archaic process.

During the evaluation, I developed a close relationship with the sales rep and her vice president of Sales. I championed hard internally for my leadership team to choose SAP

Concur, mostly because I had used the software and knew the company needed the product. At one point, my SAP Concur rep said: "Laura, you are way too excited about expense reports. I think you need to come work for us." I laughed it off and kept that thought in my back pocket for later.

The new Private Equity (PE) executive leadership team hired me, giving me a first-time, front-row seat on how PE companies operated. However, I always disagreed with the way they treated tenured staff who knew the business far better than newcomers to the team. But PE had their playbook. They would play every "X" and "O," no matter what. As a result, I often felt like a referee umpiring both sides. I wondered if both groups failed to remember basic communication rules of kindness. Forget about a playbook with X's and O's; some days felt like a boxing match with a KO (a knockout, for those unfamiliar with boxing). You just didn't know where the punch would land on your face.

The dream job I yearned for turned into a nightmare when I watched a senior sales executive publicly humiliate and berate a colleague. About twenty of us were in the conference room, and the interaction sickened me. I excused myself from the meeting and went back to my hotel room. That evening, I decided this wasn't the culture or leadership team I wanted, so I resigned a day after flying home. This was my first proper introduction, while serving in a leadership role, where my integrity and alignment with other leaders clashed. Little did I know back then how prevalent the lack of integrity would be years later when faced with other leaders behaving badly.

It was November 2015, and I didn't have a job lined up, but I was confident in my background and sales skills. I had an urge to go outside my comfort zone and become a sales rep. One of my responsibilities in sales operations was to calculate quarterly commission payouts for various sales teams. Most sales reps have an annual salary, plus variable compensation that's based on sales volume within a specific period.

Some sales reps I've supported over the years made more money in *quarterly* commission payouts than I made in an *annual* salary. I couldn't believe it. But I constantly told myself: *I can do what they do.* Eventually, I would get my chance when I started in tech sales in January 2016, after calling in that favor with my former rep at SAP Concur. I was ready to get excited about expense reports!

Before we ride that roller-coaster first year of slinging software, it's important to note that sales organizations within the tech space are their own breed. Even though I had years of experience in corporate America working directly with sales reps, being a sales rep or sales leader on the front lines in SaaS was an entirely different experience. Within sales organizations, you must know the pecking order. Hierarchies play a nuanced, political and cultural role within each sales segment. You can't dismiss them when joining a sales organization.

Working in this type of environment made it more difficult to pay it forward, but it didn't stop me from trying. I may not control someone else's decisions about corporate politics dictating their poor behavior, but I could certainly control mine. I was one person in a sales organization totaling hundreds of reps globally. I made a respectable name, differentiating myself by simply being me: trustworthy, authentic, accountable, and vulnerable. Just like my mom taught me when I was a little girl.

The Layoff Cooties – It's Them, Not You

Most software companies segment their sales teams based on the size of their potential customers within their total addressable market. They use metrics, such as annual revenue or total number of employees, to segment each market. For example:
- <$250M in revenue or 0–500 Employees = Corporate or Small Business Sales
- $250M–$1B in revenue or 501–1000 Employees = Mid-Market Sales
- >$1B in revenue or 1001+ Employees = Enterprise Sales

Each segment offers increasing levels of annual quotas for sales reps to achieve. Small business or mid-market prospective companies traditionally are paired with entry-level or less senior sales executives, while enterprise-level selling usually is reserved for more experienced reps. This is not always the case, but for the sake of understanding the dynamics within sales organizations, it's usually the most common.

My first year as a sales rep at SAP Concur was extremely challenging. I assumed I'd be able to walk right in and share my story with prospective customers about how I understood their pain points. I had just sat in their shoes evaluating travel and expense management software solutions the year before, so I had all the answers, right? Wrong. I was a bull in a china shop, disrespecting the two ears, one mouth ratio. I talked more than I listened. I blurted out features and functionality. My lack of results spoke for itself.

I sold $82K of software during my first year in SaaS sales. Nineteen percent to plan. Less than five net-new logos sold. I was in last place on my team. OK, I was in last place in my *entire* global mid-market segment. Embarrassed. Humiliated. Ashamed. That was how I felt on a good day.

I knew I was better than that. But I was trying too hard in all the wrong ways. Three times that first year, I tried to quit. One day in October 2016, I received a phone call out of the blue from a sales trainer I barely knew. She was a top sales rep for years at SAP Concur before transitioning into a coaching role on the field sales and strategy team.

She saw something in me.

She believed in me when I couldn't see it myself.

She asked if I would humble myself and start from scratch, as if I knew nothing about sales.

What did I have to lose?

My confidence was in the toilet.

I already felt like I knew nothing about sales.

So, I set aside my pride and put in the work to become the trusted advisor I aspired to be. I became curious in conversations and practiced in front of a mirror to study how my body language changed when faced with objections. I focused on the fundamentals and went back to basics. I removed myself from the outcome and allowed myself to have fun interacting with my prospects.

It didn't need to be complicated.

The following year, in 2017, I was the Mid-Market Rep of the Year, selling $1.2M of software. Two-hundred-and-sixty-seven percent to plan. Over thirty-five net-new logos sold. I achieved my annual quota in less than five months and spent the remaining seven months earning accelerated commissions and bonuses. My W-2 was over $300K. I felt validated—like I belonged.

I spent my entire SaaS career in mid-market and loved every minute because I got the best of both worlds. I helped growing organizations invest in software solutions that would catapult them to the next phase of growth, while not working with the mammoth-sized enterprise companies that often involved longer sales cycles. I was never interested in moving upmarket to be an enterprise-level seller. I earned $250–$300K or more annually in mid-market as an individually contributing sales rep, and that was fine for me. I was the CEO of my territory, managing my calendar and meeting my annual goals.

Another important fact to note. In SaaS sales, the organizations are white and male-dominated, with very little diversity in gender and ethnicity. Most are 80 percent male versus 20 percent female. There were multiple times over nearly ten years in SaaS where I was the only woman on my sales team. (What I wouldn't give to be a fly on the wall with my female sales reps out there who read that and are coyly smiling in unison. I can hear you saying: *"Preach, Sister!"*) Gender inequality became my motivation—not that I needed anything additional to spearhead my cause to be the best salesperson on my team. I always felt I had something to prove, even though my success spoke for itself.

When I interviewed for my job in 2019 at the company that would eventually lay me off four years later, I met with four white men over the course of a few weeks. At each stage of the interview process, I asked where all the women were in the sales organization. They assured me they were there, but they never gave me an opportunity to speak with any of them until after being hired. I often wondered in hindsight if part of the reason they hired me was because of my direct questioning, as it related to the lack of company diversity.

I accepted their job offer to begin employment in February 2020. My direct manager was male, as were all five sales reps other than me. I could chat about fantasy football, facial hair, and give my opinion on the best way to mow the yard, but I couldn't bring up stories about pregnancies and labor, bikini waxes or PMS symptoms. Team calls would have become uncomfortable pretty fast!

The men on my team were extremely welcoming as I was onboarding, but it would have been nice to have at least one woman on the same team, or a female mentor. Onboarding at a new company can be stressful. In sales organizations, you're expected to ramp up quickly, as there is an annual quota tied to your head count. Besides learning about the software solutions you represent, the learning curve for understanding the internal politics and dynamics between departments is just as critical to your success.

Sales is a team sport. Lone wolf sales professionals rarely succeed. Consequently, it's vital to learn who the key players are throughout an organization. Sales reps are the quarterback of every deal, meaning they are the primary contact for each prospective customer. They are the face of the company and, in my opinion, always have held the most important role because of that direct relationship.

Sales reps track and record each evaluation with a prospective company as an opportunity. They know that quarterbacking multiple sales opportunities in different phases of a buyer's evaluation can be difficult, but fun. No two deals are alike, whatever the industry, because the sales profession is a spirited ride. For months, you can work on deals with long cycle times. You nimbly create connections with multiple points of contact and different personas to win a deal. Knowing the right questions to ask prospective customers is a learned skill and was one of my greatest attributes as a top sales performer. I was never afraid to ask questions in a direct, but respectful way. This is something I practice in everyday life, and it became a respected trademark of my sales technique. Curiosity and belief are paramount to a sales professional's success, and by this stage of my career in my early forties, I exhibited the right blend of both, along with a high level of confidence.

I was quickly ramping in my new role when the world shut down in March 2020. I was in my seat for just over a month when the economic climate threw everyone off, as no one had ever experienced a global pandemic. I never worried about losing my job during the pandemic. I don't know why, but it was never anything that kept me up at night. Looking back years later, I recognize how ridiculous that sounds, but it's important to note that even during a global pandemic, I never once worried about getting laid off.

My focus that first year in 2020 was on new business sales. It's all I ever sold in my SaaS roles at previous companies. My job was to educate prospective customers who didn't already own our software and sell $600K worth of solutions to hit my annual ramped quota. I sold three deals that first year, falling short of my quota, but given the economic outlook within the global economy, I considered it a win. I was still one of the company's top performers based on my results that first year.

In December 2020, my manager approached me about a new role that focused on scaling existing customer growth. After the new year, I would be part of a founding team tasked with building out a new line of business, making history in the company. Most SaaS companies have sales teams that focus on two areas: new business and customer growth. Until this time, our company focused on new business and was losing valuable opportunities to upsell existing customers and grow that part of our company's revenues. New business sales reps each had a handful of existing customers who occasionally gained attention by upselling additional user licenses. However, if reps wanted to hit their annual quota, their make-or-break year was based on six-figure, net-new deals. Sales reps overlooked existing customers to sell directly to the new business sales teams.

Being part of a brand-new team focused on upselling existing customers in 2021 was an amazing opportunity. I immediately saw the quick wins that could occur by cultivating relationships with customers who were using our software already. Using my analytical skills from my sales operations days, I created territory plans for the entire East Coast book of business. I did this within the first month and shared it among my internal teams with a go-to-market strategy that focused on additional user licensing, bundling software packages, and completing the core solutions that customers did not yet own. I had a strategic game plan for how I was going to crush the next year. The plan worked. I achieved my annual quota in less than nine months. This meant that in the last quarter of 2021, I earned accelerated commissions for selling above my annual quota. Ka-ching! Just like my days at SAP Concur, this is where I could make the real high-dollar money.

I also created sales content and built out sales enablement resources for this new channel of customer growth business. Nearly everything our marketing teams produced up to that point focused on new business sales. An existing customer's journey differed completely from a company who never used our software. We had minimal resources, and because customer growth was such a new channel at our company, we received little support from other departments to fund our enablement initiatives. We figured it out ourselves. Well, you don't need to tell me twice! I created one-pagers, proposal decks, and value-driven business cases that concentrated on an existing customer's needs.

Being resourceful, and again using skills from my sales operations days, I paid it forward and shared the content I created with my peers to help with their sales cycles. It was a win-win situation for everyone, and I had done the hard work. I was paying it forward and sharing everything I knew with others to help catapult their success as well.

There were four customer growth sales reps in Mid-Market tasked with upselling customers that first year in 2021. My West Coast counterpart, Matt Simpson, and I on the East Coast, were making a name for ourselves as top performers throughout the entire global sales organization. Forget about what we were accomplishing within our small customer growth channel; we were setting records with higher sales than 80 percent of our new business peers! With this level of success, I felt destined to receive a well-deserved salary bump, and an increased variable compensation plan, during my upcoming performance review in December 2021.

Until I didn't. (More on that soon).

Mentoring was another way I was able to utilize my leadership skills and pay it forward. Whether I was in Sales Operations or SaaS sales, I mentored many sales reps who were in the early stages of their sales careers. Most were women. There are two main reasons I sought these opportunities:

1. I wanted to provide the mentorship I didn't receive coming through the ranks of my own sales journey. I knew how hard it was to succeed in sales, and to be a successful *woman* in sales.
2. I enjoyed learning from the younger generation as much as they enjoyed learning from me. Mentoring should be a two-way street where both parties gain knowledge, skills, and learning experiences from one another.

I saw many women come and go during my first two years at the company. Far too many women felt they didn't have the support they needed from their male managers, and from throughout the organization, to achieve long-term success. It was unfortunate. I knew several of them from previous companies where we worked together so I could attest to their previous successes. I was determined to do anything I could to help these women feel they had a place where they could pursue a rewarding career, especially the younger generation of women.

While I was only one person, I knew the ripple effect from my successes could influence others to pursue their dreams. I enjoyed building relationships and sharing my expertise and knowledge with people at work. If that's not an example of paying it forward, I don't know what is!

2 Playing the Game

Corporate America is a game. Working in a sales organization is one of the many playing fields. You either play the game or you get played. And you can't play the game without knowing all the players. There are several colleagues I'd like to introduce to you as they played pivotal roles in my four-year tenure, the events that led up to my layoff, and the lost relationships thereafter.

First Batter Up, *Annie Parks*
Annie was one of the most successful sales reps at the company before I arrived in 2020. She earned Mid-Market Rep of the Year in 2019 and was deeply respected throughout the entire company, not just the sales organization. She managed her first sales team in 2020 in Corporate New Business sales before being asked to lead the Corporate Customer Growth sales team in 2021.

I maintained a well-respected relationship with Annie. We often would commiserate about the small number of women in our sales organization and the pay inequity that existed between genders. She would do her best to hire as many women as she could on her teams to level the playing field with the rest of the sales organization. She wasn't hiring them simply because they were women; she knew if they had the right support and mentorship, they would become some of the top performing sales reps at the company. And they did.

Annie and I would pass each other handwritten notes at sales conferences to support one another. I truly believed she was an ally despite being ten years younger than me. Annie often gave me public and private praise, saying that I could be head of sales or a chief revenue officer for a major SaaS company if I wanted it badly enough. I never really aspired to setting that goal for myself, but the fact she thought highly enough of my sales acumen and leadership skills to hold such a position one day honored and humbled me.

Annie didn't mentor me directly, but I respected her position and the advice she offered, whether solicited or not. If she ever needed anything, I was happy to oblige. I can remember the Slack exchange like it was yesterday when Annie asked me to mentor Kristen. I was happy to take on another mentee that Annie thought so highly of, but I don't think either of us truly knew, at that early stage of the game, just how special Kristen would be.

Now Batting, *Rookie Kristen Miller*

How do I describe someone who had such a profound influence on me in just a short time? We were so different in so many ways. Kristen grew up on the West Coast in Southern California. I grew up on the East Coast on Long Island, New York. She graduated from a powerhouse public university at Penn State (WE ARE), and I went to the small private liberal arts school Roanoke College (GO, 'NOKE). We are nearly twenty years apart. I'm old enough to be her mother, yet she made me feel young again whenever we were together.

Our mentorship grew slowly for the first six months we worked together. I was finishing my first year in Customer Growth and she was starting her onboarding experience when she joined the company in the fall of 2021. It wasn't until the end of the first quarter of 2022 that our relationship really took off.

Kristen and I had regular one-on-one Zoom calls as part of our mentorship. She would always come prepared with an agenda she wanted to cover that ranged from basic Sales 101 questions to navigating corporate politics as a young female early in her career. No topic was off limits. We were extremely comfortable with one another and held nothing back. Considering the significant age disparity, it was a special relationship. I saw so much of myself in Kristen. Each new interaction we shared became a building block for our mentorship relationship to shift toward genuine friendship.

I trusted her.

I believed in her.

She wasn't just a colleague or a mentee.

She was a true friend.

She became a best friend.

I confided in Kristen about very serious sentiments I had about not feeling valued at work that year. Remember that annual performance review in December 2021 that didn't yield a promotion or increase in my salary and variable compensation plan? Well, I was furious that after being a top performer for two years, the company didn't take care of me financially compared with my peers.

External hires were joining the company at higher salaries and compensation plans than proven sales reps like me.

It infuriated those who remained loyal to the company. There were many grumblings about the way executive sales leadership offered higher compensation to external hires before taking care of their own.

In early 2022, I was actively looking for another job externally because I didn't feel compensated for my experience and strong sales performance. Compared with my male colleagues who had less experience and whose performance paled in comparison, I was earning less even though I was selling more than them.

It wasn't a secret that men received more pay than women. Annual salaries, signing bonuses, and variable compensation plans were greater for males than for females. Men repeatedly bragged about their salaries, and they shared compensation plans among sales professionals regularly. Talking openly about compensation was not unusual.

Sales leadership and Human Resources (HR) didn't think this was public knowledge among the sales teams, but there's a subculture where teams discuss details about compensation among teams. It was a focal point within all three sales segments of Corporate, Mid-Market, and Enterprise. Everyone knew what everyone else made.

When I was first hired, I took a pay cut compared to the company I was leaving to join their organization. I believed the corporate narrative of *"do well your first year, and we will make it up to you in year two."* I was one of the top performers in the entire company after not only one, but TWO years. The company never adjusted my salary and variable compensation plan higher, despite my global ranking as one of the top sales reps and earning the highest scores on my annual performance reviews.

Playing the Game

In 2022, I was starting with one of the lowest salaries and compensation plans across the sales organization. For someone with over twenty years in sales and a top performer, I was not happy about it. I made my grievances known to the sales leaders I believed could help me fix it. Apparently, my last manager "forgot" to push the promotion button after I received my strong annual performance review in 2021. She was no longer with the company, and the company couldn't backtrack and adjust my salary and variable compensation plan because the annual focal review period was over.

I was livid.

Why should the company penalize me for someone else's mistake?

I shared all of this with Kristen.

We had one of our deepest conversations on that day in March 2022. After our Zoom call, I sent Kristen the following Slack message:

> **Laura Krauss:**
> Hey, just wanted to say THANK YOU for listening to me earlier. I truly enjoyed our conversation. I'm a big believer that mentors learn just as much from mentees throughout the relationship. You are smart, intelligent, and have a good head on your shoulders, Kristen. Let your values be your compass and you will be successful no matter what path you choose in business. As much as Corporate America is a game that is played where we feel like a pawn, there are lifetime lessons that are learned and cannot be replicated anywhere else. I want you to know that I will always be here for you, regardless of how our

paths may wind. Please don't hesitate to reach out if you need anything at all. Have a great weekend and keep up the good work. You will continue to do amazing things!

She Slacked back, and I couldn't help but feel deeply touched with her response. She knew I was having hard conversations with sales leadership regarding my pay inequity and respected my speaking up about it. She admired my courage. This pay inequity issue would affect her one day too. She looked up to me and that felt good.

 Kristen Miller:
I have been thinking about our conversation since we got off the phone. I am so fortunate to have you as a mentor in this space because it's very rare to be able to confide in someone that you trust in a work environment, that is willing to break through boundaries and barriers and do what is right (regardless of what others think). You are truly a fighter and I admire that so much. I hope to continue to follow in your footsteps of staying true to your values. I can only imagine how challenging that continues to be as a top performing, intelligent, and compassionate woman in our industry/Corporate America as a whole. Your kids are very lucky to have a mom like you. I am always here to talk through anything as well, both positive and negative. I feel enlightened from every conversation we have, not only sales and business related, but more importantly around integrity, respect, and authenticity. Thank YOU for allowing me

> to pick your brain and bring up topics that are real. I know you never had to say 'yes' to taking on another mentee with your schedule, so please know I truly value you and your time. I look forward to the next time we chat. Have a wonderful weekend as well.

Our relationship grew extremely close throughout the end of 2022. Whenever I traveled to our New York City office, we would meet for dinners that she would organize at some of her favorite spots in the city. I would often stay at my mom's house on Long Island and commute into our New York City office where Kristen was based. Sometimes I spent the night on Kristen's couch in her apartment if our dinners and conversations went late into the evening.

One weekend in September, when I was visiting my mom, I invited Kristen out to Long Island from New York City to hang out at Robert Moses State Park beachfront. It was the local beach near where I grew up and I wanted to share some of my favorite places with her, driving past many of my old stomping grounds as a kid. I picked her up from the Babylon Station on the Long Island Rail Road, and we spent a fun morning eating bagels, sitting on the beach under overcast skies, and just talking about life.

I gifted her with a beautiful Fracture picture she had shared with me of a sunset while vacationing that summer at her Michigan lake house. On the back of the picture I printed the quote from entrepreneur and author Edmund Lee, *"Surround yourself with the dreamers and the doers, the believers and thinkers, but most of all, surround yourself with those who see greatness within you, even when you don't see it yourself."* I was always giving Kristen thoughtful gifts like these when we met up in person. I wanted her to know how special of a person she was to me and how much I valued her friendship beyond work.

Welcome Switch Hitter, *Bill Blumburgh* to the Plate

While at the beach, Kristen and I discussed the leadership opportunity the company offered me. My manager, Bill Blumburgh, was pushing hard for me to move into sales leadership. Bill was one of the first people I met when I started working there in 2020. He didn't become my manager until two years later. He worked in a customer-facing support role for several years previously. Bill understood the customer's journey more than anyone in New Business sales. Customers loved him just as much as the internal sales patriarchy did. The company hand picked him for his Customer Growth regional vice president role when my previous manager left the company for greener pastures.

Bill was at the same management level as Annie; he supported the Mid-Market segment, while Annie supported the Corporate segment. When I learned he would be my new manager in April 2022, his decision to lead our Customer Growth sales team convinced me to stay. I was no longer looking externally for another job after the December 2021 debacle of not getting my raise during the annual focal review period. I genuinely liked Bill, and we had a very trusting relationship until the last six months of my tenure. More on that later.

I was having an amazing year in 2022 as a sales rep again. Closing in on my annual quota in less than nine months for the second year in a row, I kept going back and forth on my

Playing the Game

decision to move into sales leadership. I knew it was a great opportunity. Yet, I didn't want to lose the momentum and financial benefit of achieving my quota early by taking on a leadership role three-fourths of the way through the year. I would bypass the chance to earn accelerated commissions during the final quarter of the year as I'd have to start at zero sales again as a leader. But this time, I would have a team of sales reps to support. I knew how the promotional bureaucracy worked within the walls of my company.

No interview.

No presentation.

Do you want the job?

If so, it's yours.

This is how Bill presented the leadership role to me.

The company was looking to expand the Customer Growth team by placing two new divisions under Bill's leadership. The East Coast was scaling faster with more customers. I was based in the Mid-Atlantic, and with my strong sales performance, they asked me to lead the East Coast team. Bill would continue to lead the West Coast sales reps until the right time came along to expand there as well. My colleague and fellow sales rep Matt Simpson was being targeted as the other new leader under Bill, based on his success on the West Coast.

Kristen was my sounding board. She listened to the pros and cons of moving into leadership. She was my biggest supporter and helped instill confidence in me in ways that I wasn't really prepared to hear. Specifically, she shared her belief in me and my servant-based leadership style. I accepted the leadership role and officially began my tenure as regional vice president of Customer Growth sales in

The Layoff Cooties – It's Them, Not You

mid-October 2022.

Kristen became more vocal about wanting to move to Mid-Market since I would be leading a sales team. She also wanted the challenge of selling into larger companies which Mid-Market would provide. I would have immediate openings on my team after the new year. She had been in her sales rep role in the Corporate segment under Annie for less than a year working with smaller companies, but was crushing all aspects of the job. She was on schedule to hit her annual quota early. Everyone throughout the company was well-aware of her success in her first year as a sales rep. She truly was the Rookie of the Year and received that recognition at the end of 2022.

The Real Competition, SaaS Sales Organization Politics

Remember that pecking order within sales organizations? Well, leaders within each segment tightly control their teams, especially their top-performing sales reps. Leaders make money from their team's collective performance. Training and developing sales reps is an ongoing process that is labor intensive and time consuming. When a leader gets a sales rep ramped up to speed and performing well, they want to keep them on their team for as long as possible.

Servant-based sales leaders like me, however, care just as much about the career progression of their sales reps by asking how they can best support their goals. This was not the case for most sales leaders at our company. They were possessive with their team members and our company didn't like promoting people without permission. Many times, Bill and I would get our hands slapped for merely accommodating discussions with sales reps in other segments who wanted to learn more about openings on our team. We weren't promising them a job; we were simply answering their questions about supporting our Mid-Market customers and being part of the culture in our segment. Since when did having a conversation with a colleague become unlawful?

Kristen raising her hand to be considered for a promotion from Corporate to Mid-Market and my support of that request as a brand-new sales leader caused World War III within our sales organization. Gordon Grecco, our senior vice president of sales, oversaw both the Corporate and Mid-Market sales channels. Even though they both reported up through him, he still had to manage the politics of keeping the sales leaders and their teams playing nicely in the sales sandbox. Annie and her manager lost their shit on me and Bill. Suddenly, it became this competitive battleground over a coveted, top-performing sales rep versus asking Kristen how she wanted to progress her career. I felt awful for Kristen. And I felt awful for myself too.

This scenario playing out was *exactly* why I *didn't* want to go into leadership. The political games of sales management were only just beginning. I was on the receiving end of snide remarks and rude comments at company events that alleged that I poached Kristen for my team. Mix in some alcohol at company sponsored events and you can only imagine how difficult it was for me to ignore. Gordon, Annie, and other leaders would veil the jabs in jokes, but make no mistake. They weren't joking at all. The comments were extremely hurtful to me and completely undeserved.

Everyone agreed to allow Kristen to finish out her year on Annie's team in the Corporate segment. She would officially move to my team in the new fiscal year, beginning in January 2023. The snide comments and political backlash, however, were not even close to being over.

Bill was obviously supportive of our welcoming Kristen to our Mid-Market sales team. He would benefit from having another top performer on his team, contributing toward his annual quota as a sales leader. For as much as I enjoyed working with Bill, he was also the consummate politician. He could shake hands and kiss babies like the best of them, and his laid-back style genuinely attracted people. He was, however, always looking out for himself and posturing for his next upward move on the corporate ladder. We were both excited to finish out 2022 with me leading the East Coast team as we headed into a new fiscal year.

In December 2022, our CEO announced we would no longer be a public company and agreed to be purchased by a PE firm. I had been through this exercise before when I was a sales operations manager in 2015, and more recently in 2019, at the company I had left to work here. I knew their playbook. Everything would be fine for the first couple of months. Town Halls and All Hands meetings would be held, often not sharing any real valuable pieces of information. Rumors would begin on rounds of layoffs affecting different departments. Within months, the company would dismantle the tenured executive leadership team.

For the first five months of 2023, I kept my head down and led my sales team. We finished at 95 percent to quota in Q1 and Q2 of that year. Compared with our New Business sales teams who were barely performing at 30 percent quota, I was extremely proud of our performance in a very difficult selling year. Kristen continued posting strong sales results and led my team managing a book of business of mostly New York City customers. Her customer base consisted of my former customers when I held that same role. We strategized on many deals together. The fact she was local and could visit in person with these customers certainly helped build relationships and accelerate her sales cycles.

I witnessed Kristen interacting at marketing events and in many deals with all levels of C-suites and individual contributors. She had the rare ability to speak with confidence regardless of the persona or titled executive she was meeting. Kristen asked thoughtful questions and listened intently to hear the needs of each customer. She was extremely observant, picking up on body language to pivot as needed to stay in control of conversations. I've met and worked with THOUSANDS of sales professionals over the course of my twenty-five years, and she was one of the best at her craft, especially for her limited sales experience as a twenty-six-year-old. At this pace, Kristen was on track to earning Mid-Market Rep of the Year in 2023 if she continued her journey as a sales rep on my team.

Until Bill called me on May 9th with an idea.

He and Gordon had decided they didn't want Matt to lead the West Coast team anymore. Matt had been oscillating back and forth between moving to an Enterprise sales rep role or moving into Mid-Market leadership. He wasn't doing himself any favors by not proactively helping other sales reps or thinking up new sales strategies. Bill didn't see Matt behaving like he wanted the role enough. Gordon always had a soft spot for Kristen and wanted her to move into sales leadership. And what Gordon Grecco wanted, Gordon Grecco got.

The Layoff Cooties – It's Them, Not You

I called Kristen to let her know, even though Bill wanted to tell her later that month in New York City with me in person. I knew Kristen wouldn't want to be sprung with that opportunity in the middle of our customer-facing event, which is where Bill wanted to share his and Gordon's grand idea.

I made the executive decision to call Kristen and tell her what Gordon and Bill were thinking. She was on *my* team. I had that right as her leader to present her with the opportunity, not Bill.

She was a bit taken aback, but I could tell she was excited about the opportunity.

I was really upset.

My heart sank.

I knew Kristen would jump to move into sales leadership. Annie had wanted her to think about leading a team in Corporate the previous year, which was another reason she lost her lunch on me and Bill. She wanted to mold Kristen to move into leadership in her segment; again, not asking Kristen what *she* wanted, but assuming that would be the route she would want to take. Kristen had expressed she didn't want to move into leadership after only one full year in the sales rep role, and so Annie and her boss had to honor her wishes to move to Mid-Market instead.

This timing was different, though. There were so many rumors about sales reorganization layoffs that spring and summer with the PE takeover now complete. Kristen was an individually contributing sales rep, and we were about to get more of them on our team. Her territory would shrink, and her sales opportunities would diminish. She could still have a phenomenal year and earn prestigious awards like Rep of the Year, but it would be amid a lot of internal changes within the company.

I was upset and disappointed because we couldn't finish what we had started. We barely had half a year working together and now she was being plucked to lead the West Coast team. In the back of my mind, I could see Annie grinning and happy that my tenure with Kristen on my team was now up. It was payback for her losing Kristen a few months previously. At least Annie got a full year with Kristen on her team. I got less than six months.

What I found most disturbing was that Gordon and Bill still made Matt think he was a viable selection for the West Coast Customer Growth regional vice president role. He had to create a sales deck, present it to the executive team, and formally interview for the role without knowing they were giving the position to Kristen if she wanted it.

No presentation and no interview for Kristen. Just do you want it? It's yours.

Sound familiar?

Why play games with Matt if the decision already was made to select Kristen? Because Gordon and Bill needed to control the narrative and make it look like Matt still had a viable chance. Corporate politics at its best!

Kristen and I went back and forth with the pros and cons about her moving into leadership at such a young age. Everyone was telling her to take it. I was trying to play the devil's advocate, bringing up viable concerns no one else was willing to share. I didn't think she was ready with less than six months' experience selling into Mid-Market customers, despite her initial success as a sales rep.

We would have the same role.

The Layoff Cooties – It's Them, Not You

I couldn't imagine how overwhelming of a decision that was for her. It was less than a year ago that I faced the same decision, but I had twenty more years of experience in sales than she did. I sent her a three-page manifesto documenting twenty different questions for her to consider before making her final decision.

She appreciated the thought I put into that manifesto.

But I already knew; Kristen made her choice.

Kristen knew this was devastating for me.

I convinced myself to be happy for her because it's what she wanted.

When she officially moved into the role as regional vice president of Customer Growth West in July 2023, she gave me this heartfelt, handwritten card:

When we first met almost two years ago, I knew we were going to be building something special. Did I think this mentorship would transform into a life-long friendship … not this quick. The impact you have had on me as a young woman, a professional and a friend is truly remarkable. I look up to you in so many ways: the fearless and influential woman you are in the workplace, the phenomenal mom and wife you are at home, with a fine food palate and zest for life, and the caring and genuine friend you have been to me and to others. It is truly amazing to witness and to live out the impact you have had on those around you. I truly hope I can be half the woman you are one day–your belief in others and the greater good, your earnest curiosity to get to know those around you and your uncanny commitment to your profession to getting better everyday.

> *I want to thank you for your commitment to my continuous improvement in life. I can't express in words how much FUN I have had learning from you, following in your footprints and trying to master a craft you are so phenomenal at. Yes, I have cried many times over the thought of us not tag teaming our pricing calls and strategizing on how to win over someone that buys software day in and day out! You have made this past year for us so rewarding and debatably the best year of my life. So, I thank you. From the bottom of my heart, thank you for believing in me, especially in supporting me through this most recent transition.*
>
> *While I won't/don't have 99% of the answers, there is truth in that I depend on you. "Be the woman who fixes another woman's crown, without telling the world it was crooked." You've fixed my crown many times. I cherish our friendship so much. I love sharing our food pics, recapping on our memories and just watching you in action in all ways of life (not creepy, I promise). We have YEARS of memories, vacations, and laughs to come ... and a few more breweries to hit. And a lot more NYC restaurants. I love you dearly and am so honored and humbled to have a friend like you.*
>
> *— Kristen*

With Kristen in her new role, our mentorship and working cadence simply developed organically into a newfound mutual respect. They say *the only thing constant is change*. This is true. Our friendship changed and became stronger during that time.

The Layoff Cooties – It's Them, Not You

Over the next few months, Kristen blossomed into her new role, helping to close many large deals that Bill could not get over the line when he was leading the same group of tenured sales reps. Some of it was timing with the customers, but part of it was also Kristen's sales acumen that we continued to cultivate together through our mentorship. Her team's performance in Q3 crushed mine. While I was happy for her early success in the role, I was also allowing my competitiveness to doubt my own stellar performance during the first half of the year.

Sales is competitive. In a friendly and unfriendly way.

Kristen walked into a huge pipeline with experienced and tenured sales reps, one of them being Matt, who was trying to close out his own Mid-Market book of business before transitioning to the Enterprise Customer Growth team. He had an incentive to close everything before transitioning out of the role. His performance, coupled with several other six-figure deals that were predicted for months, finally were executed in Q3 under Kristen's watch. Meanwhile, I was busy training five new sales reps who had never worked with customers before. They transitioned to my Customer Growth team from our New Business sales teams as part of the sales realignment and first round of PE layoffs in June. I was one of the few sales leaders globally who received a higher quota mid-year because of these new folks on my team.

Lucky me.

More people to manage and an inflated quota.

By October 2023, I lost two of the sales reps brought over to my team in June for greener pastures. They both confided that they weren't thrilled with being moved automatically from New Business to Customer Growth as part of the June layoff restructuring. I didn't blame them. You're either "in" or you're "out" mentally. There is no gray area in between. The stress of the PE buyout, our beloved CEO leaving earlier than expected, and this massive sales layoff and reorganization didn't make for a very fun sales culture where people wanted to stay. I could also tell from their work effort with their customer base their hearts weren't in it.

When they each put in their two weeks' notice within a month of one another, it didn't surprise me. Two-week notices at our company were really one day's notice. HR and IT work hand-in-hand to remove access as quickly as possible but usually allow time for folks to get personal documents off their laptop. I found myself down multiple sales reps and hiring all over again. Kristen had a full team of mostly tenured reps and only two New Business sales reps transitioning to her group as part of the June restructuring.

I did what I do best, putting my head down and making things happen for positive change. I immediately began asking questions when I could backfill my open head count. There was no way I could hit my ridiculously inflated sales quota the rest of the year without a full team in place. More importantly, about fifty of our customers did not have a dedicated sales rep, so they were not getting the support they needed daily.

I could only do so much with my limited bandwidth.

Knowing the internal politics that ran rampant at the company, I started vetting external candidates. The only problem was the company temporarily froze my team's head count, with no true answers on the timeline to rehire provided by Bill, Gordon, or HR. Every time I asked, I got a different answer. It was extremely frustrating. Other sales

The Layoff Cooties – It's Them, Not You

leaders were publicly posting on LinkedIn for their open positions. Even with the June layoff restructuring of the sales organization, our company was always hiring sales reps.

Why didn't the company allow me to replace my head count?

3 Game Over

Wednesdays. Nothing exciting ever happens on a Wednesday, especially the one right after Thanksgiving. I usually attend a church growth group that meets weekly at my friend Diane's house on Wednesday evenings. That Wednesday, I had a long day of virtual back-to-back meetings. This in-person Bible study group would be what my soul needed after that kind of day.

This particular Hump Day started out no differently than the typical ones when I was not traveling, visiting customers up and down the East Coast and in Canada. It was great to be home for a full week, especially because my husband Erik and I ventured north of the border to celebrate an American Thanksgiving holiday. My sister Erica lives half the year at a lake house in Val-des-Monts, in Quebec, Canada, just north of Ottawa, and this was the second American Thanksgiving in a row I spent in Canada with her.

I fulfilled my maternal duties that morning, driving our daughter, Kelsie, to school by 8 a.m., and arrived home like clockwork by 8:20 a.m. I never minded doing the drop-off for school because that meant Erik had pickup duties in the afternoon. We both benefited from the remote- work-based lifestyle for many years in our respective careers prior to

The Layoff Cooties – It's Them, Not You

the pandemic, so we had this parental/kid pickup schedule nailed down for several years. Our son, Ben, a senior in high school, drove himself to school and his many sporting activities. Lucky for him, that fall semester he was already at school by 8 a.m., so he never had to draw the short straw to drive Kelsie in the mornings.

Since there were no Thanksgiving leftovers for me to savor for breakfast, I scarfed down a healthy-sized bowl of Cap'n Crunch cereal as I read my usual news feeds on my phone at the kitchen table. Knowing I had until 9 a.m. until my first meeting, I didn't feel rushed to get back to my bedroom office, where a long day of back-to-back Zoom calls waited to greet me. I eventually made it up the stairs and fired up the old laptop in time for my first meeting of the day.

I always enjoyed my one-on-ones with Justin McFarlane. He also had a good relationship with executive sales leadership. They hand picked him to lead the East Coast New Business Mid-Market sales team after the June 2023 round of summer layoffs and restructuring. I led the Mid-Market Customer Growth sales team covering the same territory, and I upsold existing customers who were purchasing additional software solutions they didn't yet own. Justin's sales reps and mine partnered together regularly to ensure a seamless transition between sales teams. We worked with one another if his team needed a last-minute referral from our arsenal of customers. His team's success was critical to mine because our customer base grew with every new logo his team signed. Job security, baby!

"Hey Justin, how was your Thanksgiving? Did you host this year?" I asked.

Justin is a young, articulate, strategic thinker who's not afraid to sell alongside his team. I liked him a lot as we became friends when we were sales reps together before we both jumped into leadership roles in 2022. There was a mutual respect between the two of us I always appreciated.

"It was awesome, Laura."

Justin filled me in on the pleasantries of his holiday with his family. He was especially happy to have a break. He'd been traveling a lot with his team, trying to close a few deals before the holidays.

"It's been beyond frustrating lately," he said. "You know how it goes. A few of these deals have been forecasted for months now and I keep getting the verbal commitments with no signature."

Forecasting six-figure priced software is both an art and a science, even when you have a mutually aligned schedule with a prospect or customer. There are always last-minute things that pop up. It's not uncommon for a $250K deal or higher to go sideways during the last week or month in a quarter. For New Business sales reps and sales leaders, their entire quarter can ride on a few deals they've tracked for months. If one blows up, it's a morale killer for the entire organization. To say everyone vested in every deal is an understatement.

I kept shaking my head as Justin talked through his deals. "Ugh, I'm so glad I'm not selling in New Business anymore. You guys have such a tough job, especially in this market."

Morale was at an all-time low. We lost our CEO earlier that spring when he left earlier than expected after the PE buyout. Most folks thought he didn't want to be involved

The Layoff Cooties – It's Them, Not You

in the mass exodus of people via multiple rounds of layoffs for the company he built over the last nearly twenty years of his life. It was personal to him, and understandably so. He was an icon in the industry and well respected and loved by many within the organization.

"I keep hearing there's going to be another round of layoffs before the holidays," I asked. "Have you heard anything on your end?"

"Yeah, I keep hearing that too, but I'm just going to keep my head down and do what I do until I'm told differently," he said.

"Same here." I nodded in agreement.

Truth was, there's not much we could do regarding the layoffs. Tech as an industry announced layoffs regularly and our company was playing their part. In the last year, our global sales organization experienced a lot of changes to the overall corporate culture. Within each sales team, there were always grumblings of reps being put on Performance Improvement Plans (PIPs) and forced out for reasons beyond their control. Looming layoffs added to that stress in a very difficult selling climate.

On the flip side, going from a public to a private company can be an extremely lucrative situation. Many tenured folks had thousands of Restricted Stock Units or RSUs to their name (myself included). When RSUs get converted to an all-cash stock payout, the money can be life- changing. Every employee hired prior to the PE buyout received RSUs as part of their overall compensation package. Our employees benefited from an $81 per share payout, so everyone was always calculating how much money they were going to make from this public to private transaction. There was also a ton of fear in the unknown, as every PE company has their playbook for dismantling organizations in the name of operational efficiencies. It would only be a matter of time before several rounds of layoffs would affect the future of our company as we knew it.

I don't normally check my Slack messages or emails when I'm on one-on-ones. I believe in giving people my full attention so we can get through our agenda and move on with our day. But on this Wednesday, I was getting a few Slack messages from my team. I skimmed them, and there was nothing urgent, so I didn't respond right away. I glanced at a few of the email notifications popping up on my screen. My inbox was getting crowded with some customer requests, particularly around pricing proposals, tied to year-end customer renewals. There was nothing needing a reply so early in the day, so I tried to focus on my call with Justin.

Until 9:15 a.m.

The subject line of the email was only four words: Your Role Is Impacted.

What the fuck?

I couldn't believe what I was reading.

There was only one thing those four words could mean. They were laying me off.

There was a longer email body with bulleted information, but I kept focusing on those four words. The subject line on that email seemed blacker and bolder than all the other ones piling up my inbox.

My heart sank.

I felt a pit in my stomach that still aches when I put myself back in that exact moment of time. A million thoughts

The Layoff Cooties – It's Them, Not You

were going through my head. I knew I had limited time as an employee of a company I enjoyed working at for the last four years.

Justin was going on about some deal that never was going to close. I immediately interrupted. The pit in my stomach felt much deeper. My mouth was so dry, I could barely get out the words.

"Hey, Justin. I'm really sorry, but I have an emergency I need to take care of, so we'll have to catch up later."

"Oh, my goodness. Yes, of course Laura. Let me know if there's anything you need. Hope everything is OK. Chat later." I would eventually catch up with him again later and to this day, he has remained a loyal friend.

I jumped off my Zoom with Justin and immediately started reading the email again with the now infamous subject line: "Your Role Is Impacted."

This had to be a sick joke. There's no way this was happening to me. Never in a million years did I ever think a layoff would ever affect me. Even when our company had layoffs twice earlier that year, I never worried about my job. Our Customer Growth teams were scaling, and if anything, needed more leadership at the helm. Layoffs impact other people, not top performers such as myself. All the global sales organization layoffs happened in June and my Customer Growth team benefited by getting more people, not less.

How could my team lose me—their respected leader—now?

I built this channel at my company. I was a founding member of the Customer Growth sales team in 2021, leading the exponential growth on the East Coast for the first two years of the business channel. After much success, executive leadership asked me to build out an East Coast team in the first round of Customer Growth expansion. I had a stellar reputation not only with my customers, but internally. I was known for getting shit done. Not only that, I did it the *right* way. I led with trust, empathy, authenticity, and vulnerability. I mentored and trained so many reps throughout the sales organization, including sales reps outside of my Mid-Market business segment.

Leadership called on me regularly to offer advice and counsel on launching new sales processes and improving workflows. I successfully created and revamped the customer referral program with our marketing team. With my sales operations background, I brought a unique analytical skill set to the table, often helping reps with their account planning. I suggested customer sales enablement initiatives and created resources for the customer's sales journey, besides crushing my sales numbers each year. I brought in *millions* of recurring revenue to this software company over the last four years, more so than many other reps and leaders combined.

How could I be getting this awful news on what was supposed to be just a regular Wednesday?

Upon further review, Gordon sent me the email, and not HR. I remembered hearing that many of the layoff emails from earlier in the year came from someone in HR. Why was my communication coming directly from Gordon?

Dear Laura,

I'm writing to inform you that your role has been impacted by workforce changes and that a separation is pending.

Here's what to expect:

You'll receive a calendar invite from me with the subject, "Meeting," where I'll detail next steps.

In that meeting, I'll need to confirm your personal email address to ensure you receive separation materials.

Your access to company-sensitive systems will be restricted; however, you will still have access to your Google drive and G-suite, MyHR, and other day-to-day productivity apps through the end of today.

Based on company protocol, physical access also will be limited. Should you need access to an office, please let me know.

Our focus now is ensuring that you're treated fairly as you depart and support you as you bridge to your next career opportunity.

Losing a job is extraordinarily hard. That's why we want to provide you with as much support as possible. In the materials to follow our meeting, you'll see separation package details. This includes a cash severance payment, paid health benefits where applicable, partial cash-award equity acceleration, and extended access to the Employee Assistance Program.

To keep an open line of communication, we set up region-specific help desks staffed by the People team to address your questions or concerns. Contact information will be in those materials, as well.

You made a difference and your contributions are appreciated.

You helped to make this a more vibrant community and more successful company. You'll always be a part of our story and a valuable member of our alumni.

Thank you, Gordon

How boilerplate of a termination email can someone get?

It was now almost 9:30 a.m. Even though I had read the message several times over, my self-preservation instincts kicked in. I had limited time. The meeting Gordon referenced was now on my calendar, ready to be accepted. It was scheduled for 10:45 a.m., and I believed he and someone from HR would be on that call.

I immediately called Kristen. She was traveling that week, supporting reps on her West Coast team, so it was only 6:30 a.m. I knew she had a full day visiting with a customer, but I figured she might be up early getting ready. The first call went straight to her voicemail. I hung up. I called again, and this time she answered.

"I just got laid off!" I yelled into the phone. "Can you believe this? What the *fuck* is going on?"

The Layoff Cooties – It's Them, Not You

I could tell I woke her because she groggily answered. "Wait a minute, Laura. What?"

"I just *fucking* got laid off!" I was screaming into the phone. My heart felt like it was beating outside of my chest. She didn't deserve to be on the other end of my anger, but I had to get it out.

"What do you mean, you got laid off?" she said.

I recounted the pieces of the last hour. The call with Justin, the email, the calendar invite.

"But that doesn't make any sense." Kristen was still half asleep and trying to figure out what the hell was going on.

Tell me about it, I thought.

I needed to get off the phone. My time as a regional vice president of Customer Growth Sales was ticking away.

"I'll call you later. I need to go." I quickly hung up with her and sprang into action.

Typically, when folks are let go, access to email and main systems are available until 5 p.m. Gordon's email said I would have access through the end of the day too, so I didn't immediately think to save my personal documents and files I stored on my company-issued laptop. Hindsight is twenty-twenty. I never should have had any personal documents on my work computer, but I didn't have my own laptop, so I kept everything on my work computer within our Google drives.

My meeting with Gordon was less than an hour away. I wasn't concerned with anyone else affected by this round of layoffs. I didn't reach out to my team during that next hour. I couldn't change the decision obviously made behind closed doors weeks or days prior to me receiving this blindsiding communication.

One of the worst things about being laid off is that you're never able to say goodbye on your terms. There are no virtual happy hours or time to celebrate the myriad of collective achievements with coworkers. The company controlled the narrative and communication. Often, colleagues don't even know you're gone until they don't see your name anymore on the Slack channel.

This couldn't happen to me, I thought. I deserved more respect than that. I wanted to exert whatever control I had left in my limited time, so I forwarded my layoff email to the brand-new CEO and CCO, two executives I thought could save me from this nightmare:

> Good morning,
>
> I am deeply saddened to not be able to continue the important work that I have dedicated myself to over the last nearly four years. This separation notification is extremely surprising given the performance of my team being one of the best and given the personal contributions as one of the top performers throughout Mid-Market when I was in those roles.
>
> I am undoubtedly shaken but my faith assures me this will lead to greater things to come.
>
> I can't help but feel that my recent communications with my direct leadership team where I vulnerably shared areas of personal and professional growth were taken out of context. I am a servant leader

and will always do what is best for the greater good of my team. I plan to attend the requested call with Gordon Grecco at 10:45 am EST today and will share these concerns at that time.

I wish you all the best. I am proud of the legacy I leave behind and appreciate your role as part of our joint story.

Best, Laura

I also blind-copied about a hundred of my colleagues on this outreach. Gordon, Bill, and Annie purposefully weren't on the email chain. I'm sure there were folks I inadvertently left off the distribution list, but this was the most comprehensive list I could compile in the limited time before my meeting with Gordon.

The pit in my stomach continued to ache. Clearly, that one bowl of Cap'n Crunch was not sufficient for this unexpectedly stressful Wednesday morning. I didn't know what to do with myself for the next twenty-four minutes. My mind wandered, and I kept rereading the termination email.

Ten minutes to go until my call with Gordon. My phone pinged again with another text at 10:34 a.m. This time, it was from Bill:

> I am learning this at a nearly identical time as you are. Feel free to call if you'd like.

Seriously?

I was absolutely furious. He had the audacity to text me that message? He knew I'd be on a call with Gordon in eleven minutes. (Bill was *not* learning about this in *nearly identical timing*, and I'll unpack that in a later chapter). Once again, Bill was trying to play Mr. Politician and control the narrative so he would come out unscathed as an unknowing and unwilling participant in my layoff. The company stripped my livelihood from me just an hour ago, and he's texting *me* so I can call *him*? WTF. What an asshole!

OK, buddy. Let me put that on my "to do list." Call Bill when I am "free." Fuck you. You still have your candy-ass job doing absolutely nothing to create value for our team.

As first-line sales leaders, Kristen and I closed the deals with our sales reps, and everyone in our sales organization knew it. Bill played politics all day from his cushy home office. Bill knew this was happening to me and did nothing. He preserved himself in this mess. I couldn't give Bill any more thought. My call with Gordon was less than ten minutes away, and I needed to think clearly.

I went back to my email and read through some of the other messages in my inbox. Why? I don't know. It's not like they mattered. Those customer emails were someone else's problem. I quickly glanced at my Slack channel and while messages were there too, I clicked on them but didn't really process what any had to say. Time felt like it stopped, but kept speeding up at the same time. My heart was racing and that pit in my stomach felt more nauseating with each passing second.

Then 10:45 a.m. came.

I logged into the Zoom call only to notice that Gordon's camera wasn't showing his face. There was some stupid picture of a nature scene populating the center of that black box on the left-hand side of my screen. On the right-hand side, I was fully visible in my pale pink cardigan sweater, looking straight into the camera.

Gordon was always on camera for Zoom calls. He never misses an opportunity to be front and center. HR was nowhere to be found. There was no third box on the screen. Unless Gordon was visiting one of our global offices with HR in the backdrop, I assumed he was delivering this message from his home office in Canada. It didn't matter where the hell he was sitting; he was disrespecting our conversation by not turning his camera on, and it pissed me off.

"Gordon, can you please turn on your camera to do this?" I said with confidence.

He laughed. "Sorry, Laura. No, I can't. It's not working today."

"Oh, how convenient for you," I replied.

I'd later find out his camera was working just fine when he told my team later that morning that I was no longer their leader.

"Laura, I'm really sorry to have to do this, but your role has been eliminated and today is your final day with us. You're eligible for severance, including health insurance. It's the standard package. Make sure we have your personal email on file so we can send you all the follow-up details because your access will be turned off later today."

I jotted down notes as he talked, but I had so many questions.

"Who's replacing me?" I expected him to say Bill or Kristen.

"The role is eliminated, so no one is replacing you. I really can't answer any more questions. Oh, wait ... I'm just learning now that you sent an email to a bunch of people letting them know you were laid off. I wish you hadn't done that."

In hindsight, I should have sent the goodbye email later in the day, *after* I retrieved my personal files from my laptop. Within the next five minutes, the company denied my access. Email. Slack. Salesforce. Google Drive. Gone. My company shut down my access like I was a white-collar criminal.

And that was it.

In less than four minutes, my entire four-year tenure was over. By 11 a.m., Laura Krauss was officially and physically kicked off the server and network. I logged off for the final time, shutting down my laptop.

I sat there in disbelief at the disrespect Gordon had shown me.

This was the guy who hired me four years prior.

This was the guy I enjoyed drinks with at company events.

This was the guy who met my family on President's Club trips to Hawaii and Cancun.

This was the guy who decided I was no longer part of his future leadership team.

This was the guy who was such a coward he couldn't even turn on his video camera for less than five minutes to thank one of his most productive and highest achieving sales professionals.

This was the guy who cared more about protecting his ego than answering my questions.

This was the guy who was single-handedly responsible for my layoff.

Without a doubt, sending my goodbye email to over one-hundred colleagues before my call with Gordon affected when the company shut down access to my laptop. My emotions on that traumatic morning got the best of me, and in retrospect, it's one of my biggest faux pas. I don't regret sending the email; I simply regret the timing of doing so before removing my personal documents from the server.

Shortly after I sent that email, I received text messages and voicemails from many of the people I blind-copied on that communication. I was happy they heard the news of my layoff directly from me, even though there was nothing I could do about the final decision to let me go. My colleagues supported me in their outreach on the day of my layoff; it was amazing. It wasn't until the dust settled a few weeks later that I noticed the deliberate lack of engagement and response when I would reach out, especially with my direct team.

I sent the screenshot of that ridiculous text I received from Bill over to Kristen. I knew she had a busy day out in the field with one of her sales reps. She's really good at compartmentalizing things, so even though I knew she was very upset by my early morning news, I was happy to know she was staying busy until we could connect again later that day. A few hours later she texted:

KRISTEN: Still here ... checking in.

ME: I'm OK. The amount of people reaching out has been humbling and very kind.

Game Over

> KRISTEN: This is going to shake up and touch people personally. You are very loved, Laura.

> ME: I feel it. Thank you.

> KRISTEN: Makes no sense to me. I'm so upset.

> ME: I'm sorry.

> KRISTEN: You mean so much to me Laura.

> ME: Thank you Kristen. I know. The feeling is mutual. Believe me. Best part of my working here was meeting you. Truly. You've helped me in ways you'll never know. We got this. Believe.

> KRISTEN: We have life, always, Laura. The best part of my day was talking to you and learning from you. Professionally always, but personally I admire you and have the utmost respect and love for you and your family. You have impacted my life so much.

The Layoff Cooties – It's Them, Not You

> **ME:** Well I have a lot more life to live as do you 20 years behind. But I look forward to being part of all your exciting life moments. I genuinely smile every time I see a text come through from you.

> **KRISTEN:** I smile with you always! And I mean that.

I sat in my bedroom office wondering what to do next. Erik was working downstairs, and I wasn't in the right mindset to tell him what had transpired that morning. He was busy with his clients on back-to-back calls, and the last thing he needed was this bad news to bombard him when he had several billable hours of work ahead. I decided not to tell him my big news until later. But I wasn't sure when "later" would be. I sent a final text to my team around lunch time:

> **ME:** I wish you all the very best. I hope you'll always remember how I fought for our team every single day. It was my greatest honor being your fearless leader. Thank you for your dedication to making yourselves better. Pls lmk if I can help any of you as you continue on your professional sales journey. I'm always here if you want a listening ear or if you need reminding of the #UntappedPotential that lives in each of you. Have a great holiday season and I hope our paths cross again one day soon!

> MY TEAM'S TEXT: Your leadership has been great and we appreciate the encouragement. So sorry to hear the news Laura. You will be a huge success no matter where you go. This is so shocking. We greatly appreciate all that you put into this team and this company!

Why did I feel like I was letting my team down? This was not my decision. We were building something special, and I wouldn't finish out the fiscal year with them. At that point, it dawned on me that I was also going to lose a ton of money.

Based on my termination date of November 29, 2023, I would receive commissions through November. The company still had December and January to close out the books, which usually were the highest grossing months at fiscal year-end. I knew my team had $2M in the pipeline, plus additional deals that would be generated in the final weeks from year-end incentives. Our customer growth team typically closed 60 percent of our pipeline, so that was a commission on $1.2M in sales that I would be screwed from getting. This equated to tens of thousands of dollars based on my variable compensation plan.

I had invested deeply that year to build this pipeline with a myriad of reps that were thrown on my team just months before. I did the *hard work* of cultivating a high-performing, fun culture with our team that was getting sales results in a tough economic climate. I felt so disrespected on so many levels.

The Layoff Cooties – It's Them, Not You

First, with an email communicating my termination.

Second, with a faceless senior executive sales leader at my Zoom meeting.

Third, with the realization all my personal documents were unretrievable.

Fourth, with the understanding a year's worth of work and pipeline building would not be compensated.

And fifth, with the anger, disappointment, embarrassment, humiliation, and shame that my layoff created.

And that was just my initial feelings in less than a few hours!

I cried for the first time.

Sitting at my desk staring at my closed laptop was not doing me any favors. I had to talk to someone. But who should I call? No way was I calling my eighty-one-year-old mom. I didn't need her to worry. I have three brothers and a sister, but I didn't want to call any of them either. I wasn't ready for my sister's wrath toward corporate America quite yet. That would come later, as she loves to lament the perils of working for big, bad corporations. She spent her entire career in public education and academia. Yeah, OK, like that bureaucracy is not as messed up as the business world? I wasn't in the mood. One brother was a lawyer; he was in real estate and probably knew little about employment law. My two other brothers were retired from public service and a middle school special education teacher, respectively. Not the kind of support I was looking for. Plus, it was the middle of the day; they were busy. At least, that's what I told myself.

I called my friend Diane, who led my Wednesday night Bible study group. Our entire group knew how important my career was to me because I'd often bring up work-related stories as part of our faith-based discussions. They knew Gordon, Bill, Kristen, and the rest of my team through months of storytelling. Yes, Diane would be the perfect person to call. She would understand and know exactly what to say. I dialed her number.

"Hey Diane, it's Laura. Do you have a minute?" In hindsight, that seemed like a stupid question. I needed more than a minute. My life was falling apart.

"Hey, Laura! Yes, of course. What's up?"

"I just got laid off." I realized that was the first time I calmly said it out loud, and not screaming into the phone like I did with Kristen a few hours earlier. In a short period of time, my emotions fell from the highs of shock, rage, and anger. I would learn very quickly that the stages of grief are not linear. You don't progress from one to another in a straight line and in a specific amount of time. I felt many grief stages at once before a calmness settled over me. It was new territory for me to manage. It was traumatic.

"Oh, my goodness. I'm so sorry. Are you OK?" Diane is one of the most sincere people you could ever meet. I could hear her genuine concern coming through the phone.

"Yeah, I think I'm still in shock. Erik's working downstairs, and I haven't told him yet. I'm already locked out of everything on my laptop. So, I'm just sitting in my bedroom office right now, trying to figure out my next move."

"Laura, I am so, so sorry. I can't believe this. You're an amazing leader. What can I do to help?"

I honestly didn't know what to tell her. She offered to say a prayer together, and that's what we did. I wish I could remember the exact words of her prayer, but by the end of it I was hunched over and bawling my eyes out. Through

The Layoff Cooties – It's Them, Not You

my sobbing, I thanked her and told Diane I would see her later that night.

It was Wednesday, after all.

Except now there was nothing normal about it.

4 Shock—This Can't Be Happening

I didn't tell Erik the company laid me off. Not on the day it happened. I needed to be in the right mindset. I needed him to be in the right mindset too. Telling him during the middle of his busy workday wasn't the right time or place. Over twenty-five years together (and a little bit of common sense) taught me that much.

Erik is my steady Eddie. He is temperate and maintains a calm demeanor; nothing gets him too high or too low. This is a good thing because I am an emotional roller coaster. We've been that way since we first met in July 1999.

I was living in Roslyn, Virginia and interning in the U.S. Chamber of Commerce the summer before my senior year of college. Erik was working as a CPA and living in Maryland with a few of his friends. Our mutual friend Kara had a birthday party at her townhouse in Springfield, Virginia, and we both attended. Kara and I went to college together, playing on the soccer and lacrosse teams and pledging the same sorority, Chi Omega. She was three years older than me, and we became close my freshman year. Kara and Erik graduated high school together and were connected through other mutual friends who came to the same party. I was the youngest person in the crowd, as most of Kara and her roommate's friend group were in their mid-twenties and older. Erik and I found ourselves alone on the back deck, talking until 3:00 a.m.

I woke up Kara shortly after Erik left, telling her how excited I was to meet him, lamenting over why she didn't introduce us earlier. Whether she was half asleep or really meant it, she jokingly said, "No way!" Later that day, I called my mom telling her I met the guy I was going to marry. I never talked like that. I barely brought a boyfriend home for my parents to meet. She gave me the same laughing response: "No way!" The rest is history.

I knew Erik would be supportive, but I couldn't face him that evening after his workday ended. There wasn't much time anyway. Erik was on calls with clients until 5:30 p.m., and I had to leave for my Bible study class by 6:00 p.m.

I was ashamed.

I was embarrassed.

I was feeling guilty, as though I let our family down.

I attended Wednesday night's Bible study class at Diane's as planned and came home by 9:00 p.m. as usual. I kept myself busy doing a few chores around the house, trying to minimize conversations and stay out of my family's way. My laptop was still on my desk in my bedroom office, so nothing was out of the ordinary for Erik to think anything unusual happened. Erik went to bed around 10:00 p.m., and I found myself in my son's bedroom having small talk before he turned in for the school night.

The stress and enormity of that day suddenly rushed over me like a tsunami.

"I lost my job today, Ben." I immediately broke down. It was like the floodgate opened and Niagara Falls cascaded down my face.

Shock—This Can't Be Happening

"Oh my goodness, Mom. I'm so sorry." Ben hugged me, holding me close as I sobbed into his athletic shoulders and arms.

Who was this man that I had raised who was now comforting me the way I did when he was younger?

No longer a little boy, but graduating soon from high school, Ben consoled me in a way that was so tender and dear I wouldn't have wanted it any other way.

I shared with him the details of how I was let go earlier that day. The feelings of disrespect, disappointment, shame, and anger were still very much a part of my frustration as I recounted the play-by-play.

"Mom, you are one of the strongest people I know. You have always supported our family, and we couldn't be more proud of you. You will get another job. You will bounce back from this. I know it doesn't seem like it right now, but you will be OK. We will all be OK." I believed everything he said, but it still didn't diminish my deep feelings of loss.

"I know. I just ... I just really loved my job. And to have someone else take that away from me just feels ... it just feels so unfair." I kept wiping away the tears on my shirt.

"Have you told Dad yet?" he asked.

"No, and I haven't said anything to Kelsie either, but I will tomorrow."

"OK, well, your secret is safe with me. Just please stop crying, Mom. I hate seeing you like this. I love you."

Ben was born an old soul. When Erik and I told him at age five that he was going to be a big brother, he looked directly at each of us and asked, "Does this mean you won't love me anymore?"

Ugh. Dagger in the heart.

The Layoff Cooties – It's Them, Not You

We reassured him. "No, Ben. It means we love you even more because we wanted you to have a sibling."

Ben was always the protective big brother to Kelsie once she was born. And in this moment of my imploding grief, he was protecting me too.

Erik was supposed to drive Kelsie to school the next day, but I told him my calendar cleared up and I could take her.

Well, that wasn't a lie, was it?

Before Kelsie and I left for school that morning, I left a note on Erik's desk in his office. Mr. Routine was always at his desk by 8:15 a.m. so I knew he would read it before I returned home. My mom always told me to put dates on everything, so I included November 30, 2023 in the upper right-hand corner. It wasn't lost on me that I wrote my message on a UNICO Riviera Maya Hotel piece of paper. It was the notepad I took from the last President's Club trip we attended in Cancun, Mexico, earlier in the year to celebrate my stellar sales performance. I wrote in all caps:

ERIK,

I WAS NOTIFIED YESTERDAY THAT MY ROLE HAS BEEN ELIMINATED AS PART OF THE PE ACQUISITION. I AM RECEIVING A SEVERANCE PACKAGE. THIS IS A SHOCK TO MY SYSTEM AS IT FEELS LIKE A DEATH, BUT MY FAITH IS STRONG AND YOU KNOW I WILL LAND ON MY FEET. GOD IS GOOD AND WE ARE BLESSED. I APPRECIATE YOUR LOVING SUPPORT DURING THIS DIFFICULT TIME.

 ME

Shock—This Can't Be Happening

Behind my handwritten note was a copy of the severance agreement and COBRA health insurance paperwork. I knew he wouldn't read through the pages of minutia that morning, but like a good CPA's wife, I wanted to ensure he had the documentation when he was ready to review it in greater detail.

While I drove Kelsie to school, I told her I had lost my job. She was sitting in the passenger seat next to me and a tear started in her left eye.

"Are we going to have to move?" She looked over in my direction.

"Why would you ask that, Kelsie? Of course not." I guess I shouldn't have been too surprised by her question. One of her friend's parents had lost his job recently, and the family moved to a different state. It was a normal reaction for a kid her age. "No, we don't have to move, but I am going to take some time before deciding what I want to do next with my career. The holidays are right around the corner, so let's just agree to make it the best Christmas ever, OK?" I was trying to convince my little girl her world (and mine) wasn't falling apart.

Kelsie's favorite holiday was Christmas. Even though at eleven years old she didn't believe anymore in Santa, she loved the family traditions we kept. I needed to make sure the timing of my layoff wouldn't ruin our Christmas and New Year holidays.

When I arrived home, I parked my Jeep in the usual spot and sat for a few minutes with my eyes closed, breathing in and out. I told myself: *today is going to be a good day.* I walked in the side door by the garage, through the laundry room foyer, and into the kitchen to see Erik walking from his office to meet me. He smiled and opened his arms wide.

There was nowhere else I needed to be at that moment than in the comfort of my husband's arms. He must have passed that quality onto Ben because less than twelve hours earlier, I received the same loving embrace.

This is what matters in life, Laura. For years, you've been so concerned about your professional legacy, and while that has its place, the more important things in life are your personal legacy.

Erik.

Ben.

Kelsie.

Me.

That's all that matters.

Now and forever.

My family was doing their part to help me get through this awful experience. Now I needed to do my part to help myself.

Ironically, sales is about helping people. Well, at least when it's done right. Prospects and customers have a business problem, and sales professionals have a potential solution. I was skilled in helping prospects and customers find business solutions. It was like a puzzle. Give me a few pieces and let me ask some direct questions. Yes, we'll find a solution together. I was determined to find the answer to my problem and complete this disturbing puzzle.

Why was I laid off?

I thought about the events that transpired during the days, weeks, and months before I received that shocking 9:15 a.m. email notification. My former company laid off other folks that same day, but it was much smaller in number than the previous layoffs. These layoffs appeared more targeted, meaning there weren't full teams being let go. It

Shock—This Can't Be Happening

was a person here and another person there. I was the only sales leader laid off this round. In fact, I was the only person in Mid-Market that was laid off.

The timing didn't make sense. Not that there is ever a *good* time to get laid off, but laying off me, with my sales leader position, didn't make sense. Why now? We had two months to finish out the fiscal year, which were the busiest and most profitable months. Any changes to the organizational sales structure wouldn't be made until February 2024 at the earliest. Sales organization layoffs happened during the summer of 2023, so why wasn't I part of that group if they knew my role was going to be eliminated?

I started thinking about the day before my layoff to see if anything was out of the ordinary.

As I was preparing to log off my laptop the Tuesday night before, Kristen sent me an odd sequence of Slack messages. She described a meeting Bill quickly had put on her calendar for the next day that made little sense to her. (*This* is the meeting I was referencing in the last chapter letting me know Bill knew about my layoff before that morning). It was unusual because Bill also sent a calendar invite to Gordon at the same time but under a separate invitation. Kristen was letting her imagination get the best of her because of the impromptu meetings popping up with her team and Gordon's.

Kristen loved scoping out people's calendars, trying to fish out any information she could find. She used to send me screenshots of other leader's schedules alerting me of things she found out simply from her calendar curiosity. That's probably what made her a great sales professional. ABC. In the sales world, ABC means Always Be Closing, but I like to say, Always Be Curious.

The Layoff Cooties – It's Them, Not You

Kristen was excellent at closing deals and being curious. There wasn't anything wrong with what she was doing. If people keep their calendars open with a public setting for anyone to view, they shouldn't be too concerned about who can see their meetings. I took a peek myself after she voiced her concern about the call Bill had scheduled with her team. I noted there was nothing on my calendar with Bill or Gordon.

Our sales reps were always uneasy about layoffs since the announcement we were moving from a public company to a private one. Both Kristen and I were fielding questions constantly from our teams about layoff rumors permeating the sales organization. We would assure them each time that our Customer Growth teams were increasing in number, not decreasing, and the best thing we could do was to put our heads down and focus on supporting our customers. This was the first time, however, that I heard Kristen legitimately nervous about *her* job.

> KRISTEN: I just want to know if I am being pushed out of a job.

> ME: I don't think you are.

> KRISTEN: OK, OK. I am overthinking.

> ME: Kristen, they wanted YOU for this job, remember? You've crushed it immediately. You are totally fine.

> KRISTEN: But Bill is probably trying to save himself too. Ya know.

> ME: And even if you are pushed out ... YOU WILL LAND ON YOUR FEET in a better position. Which I don't think you are being pushed out.

> KRISTEN: Yes. You are RIGHT. Always.

> ME: Besides, you HAVE to land somewhere—so you can hire me one day.

> KRISTEN: OK but we might be baristas.

Kristen and I spoke on the phone later that night.

"Are you sure Bill said my team would be getting a calendar invite too?" I asked her. I had my regular team call at 11:00 a.m. on Wednesday, but he hardly ever joined us each week.

"Yes, 100 percent positive," she responded. "It's so weird, Laura. Bill and I had a chat about the customer appreciation dinners we're doing and he was like, 'Oh and tomorrow, we will have a quick sync on performance and pending deals and yada, yada, yada.' And it was very odd. This meeting is really throwing me off."

The Layoff Cooties – It's Them, Not You

I knew Kristen was overreacting about this meeting being on her calendar. As a new sales leader, her confidence could be shaken easily. I enjoyed playing Mama Bear in our roles.

"I know it has you jolted," I said. "You have two choices. You can call Bill and ask him about what you see on the calendar with Gordon, or you can just wait until tomorrow."

"I am going to wait. Patiently impatient," she said with a laugh.

It all made sense now. The Wednesday meeting at 11:00 a.m. Bill placed on Kristen's calendar the previous day was planned meticulously by him and Gordon. It included Kristen's full team of West Coast reps, along with my East Coast reps, who were added shortly before the call. Gordon would join the call a few minutes after everyone was there to share the big news of my immediate departure. No wonder Gordon kept our call at 10:45 a.m. brief. He would tell my team the shocking news minutes after our Zoom meeting. (I learned later that Gordon's Zoom camera worked fine for that 11 a.m. meeting, but was inoperable for mine).

I took the news of my layoff to LinkedIn on Friday, December 1, 2023. I started typing, letting the emotions seep out of every vulnerable bone in my body. I wanted to let the world know what happened while intentionally crafting a gracious message. I loved the company I dedicated myself to for the last four years. I literally bled their company colors. It pained me to no longer work there. I needed everyone to know the impact it was having on me.

I also wanted folks to know that the sales leadership targeted me. I wrote the words delicately, but make no mistake about it. My layoff was politically motivated. You'll learn more in the next few chapters why I believe this is true.

You can decide for yourself, but the events that transpired weeks before my layoff were more than coincidental.

Pushing the POST button on LinkedIn made it real. My post read:

"What I'd want you to know ...

My time was extinguished on 11/29 at 9:15 am when I received a 'Your Role Is Impacted' email. For those that have never experienced this, consider yourself lucky. I can still feel the pit in my stomach when I had to tell a colleague on Zoom I needed to deal with an emergency. You see, up until age 45, leaving my employer was always my decision—not theirs.

Prior to our new CEO's start date in November, she sent a charismatic video introducing herself and sharing her excitement for the next chapter in her career. I admit to watching that first video at least 5-6 times.

Her outreach specifically requested wanting to meet 1:1 with as many employees as possible during her onboarding. What impressed me most about her humble personality was her genuine interest in learning more about what mattered to each of us. In turn, she wanted us to know about her.

Realizing getting on her calendar would take time, I was in the process of creating a video outreach to introduce myself and my amazing team of sales professionals when my tenure prematurely expired.

So here's what I'd want her to know if I had the opportunity to meet with her 1-1 TODAY.

I'd want her to know that I started my journey in 2020 closing my first Mid-Market New Business deal in six months' time before being asked to pilot the first Mid-Market Customer Growth team in 2021. No one knew at the time just how much of a success Customer Growth would be, but my partner in crime Matt Simpson and I both had fun figuring it out, competing against one another to hit our annual quotas by the end of Q3. Mission Accomplished. We rolled it back in 2022 repeating that same feat before I was asked to lead a carousel of talented sales professionals in Mid-Market East.

I'd want her to know that I absolutely LOVED my job and for the first time felt like I was in the role that my 25 years of sales experience had cultivated. My decision to not move into leadership earlier in my career was due to my growing family and I did not want to be away from them with all the travel requirements. I'd want her to know my leadership experience was cut short not by my choice, but by a select one or two who took my vulnerable feedback and decided it would be easier to let me go then answer questions around requests for equitable pay and timing on backfilling my open head count.

Shock—This Can't Be Happening

Finally, I'd want her to know that while I'm still working through the spectrum of emotions one would expect with such an untimely and surprising notification, I am so GRATEFUL and BLESSED for the relationships built over the last four years, the challenges that were overcome together, the welcoming mentorship I was able to provide to countless others, and the daily laughs that were shared.

My heartbeat runs through the Customer Growth teams. I wish nothing but the best for all in my wake. My greatest fear is being forgotten. Please keep in touch!"

The immediate outpouring of support from this public declaration yielded the exact response I anticipated and needed to cheer me up. I had a strong reputation with customers, colleagues, and partners within my business network, and it felt good to read their comments to this heartfelt post.

It's important to note at this time, just days after my layoff, I didn't feel like I had the layoff cooties yet. The layoff was too fresh. The impact of my departure shocked everyone else as much as it shocked me. It wasn't until the following week, when I reached out to several members of my direct team, and to Kristen specifically, when I felt they avoided me like the plague.

The layoff cooties plague.

I wouldn't wish it on anyone.

I would soon learn just how common a disease this was. You know.

The Layoff Cooties – It's Them, Not You

You've been there.
You know how contagious it can be.
Not shocking at all.

5 Denial—Top Performers Don't Get Laid Off

My own biases formed over twenty-five years in corporate America leaned heavily on the belief that top performers don't get laid off. It simply didn't happen. Why would any company want to get rid of someone in sales who was bringing in millions of revenue for their bottom-line year in and year out?

I viewed denial as a two-way street:
1. Denial that comes with grief.
2. Denial of the reality of layoffs impacting me and my team.

Both needed to be unpacked.

Denial is different from not understanding. Denial is a defense mechanism during which a person (me) refuses to accept the reality of a situation (my layoff). It's designed to help protect against the shock. Here's the thing. I never refused to accept the reality of my layoff. It was very clear. One day, I had a job. The next day, I didn't. Not much to deny there, right? I wasn't refusing or avoiding the topic of my layoff in conversation. If anything, it's ALL I wanted to talk about. I never shied away from trying to figure it all out. And in my mind, that wasn't correlating with anything related to being in denial.

The Layoff Cooties – It's Them, Not You

Our entire sales organization had so much churn at every level. With long sales cycles and unrealistic, activity-based metrics and expectations, most reps didn't stay longer than eighteen months. I used to keep a spreadsheet with everyone in Corporate and Mid-Market's performance in the four years I was there. I also kept track of their tenure. I can't tell you how many times I updated that spreadsheet throughout the year with new names of sales reps and leaders moving in and out of their roles because of performance issues. This was mostly on the New Business side of the sales organization.

Our Customer Growth teams saw greater levels of success and tenure among our teams; it's not that one was better than the other. It was a very different selling process and relationship that we had with our existing customer base. We closed a much higher percentage of business and at more regular intervals throughout the months and quarters. Seeing people win fuels morale. Winning often has the same effect. We cultivated that on our Customer Growth teams with the fun culture and leadership I created—both as a top sales rep and later as a top sales leader. During previous rounds of layoffs, we never worried that anyone on our Customer Growth team would be affected. With our team's previous successes, there was no need for me to feel like my job was ever in jeopardy.

I never wanted to move into a sales leadership role before this experience. At previous companies, my managers would inquire as to my career goals. I was having too much fun and making too much money as an individual contributor to think about the stress and management of multiple sales personnel. I hated corporate politics and while I knew the game had to be played, if I stayed in an individual contributing

Denial—Top Performers Don't Get Laid Off

role, I could minimize the amount of politics in my average day to day. For the bulk of my software sales career, this game plan worked well. While I never was shy giving my opinions to senior-level management, overall I navigated the political waters without too many bureaucratic ripples.

I'm an all-or-nothing-type of person and knew if I made the move to leading a team, I needed all the resources available to me. This meant building out my team and hiring the people I wanted to hire. Little did I know, when I transitioned to the leadership role in mid-October 2022, I would never receive the promised resources for the job they hired me to do.

I had a few openings on my team, even with Kristen joining at the start of the new year. I interviewed external candidates and realized very quickly the hiring requirements tied to my open Customer Growth roles were being held to the same standards as New Business hires. The skill set for working with existing customers differs from the skill set for prospecting net new business. I had performed both roles, and while much of my sales acumen could be utilized, there were key differences I learned on the fly that were critical to my success from New Business to Customer Growth. I wanted the freedom to hire who I felt was best suited for the role. As we began the interview process with multiple candidates, I could tell very quickly that I was going to have to fight for who I wanted.

Perhaps companies should give boxing gloves to new sales leaders to prepare them for such fights. I was ill-prepared for the myriad of hiring politics that soon ensued.

Left punch. Right punch. Gut punch. Sucker punch.

It seemed to be one right after the other.

The Layoff Cooties – It's Them, Not You

It was clear I didn't have the final say in who I could hire.

Several candidates made it through the first few rounds of interviews with me, receiving excellent feedback and recommendations for hire. One candidate worked previously with Matt and came as a referral. Matt was highly regarded at our company, so the fact he referred her should have carried additional weight. She and I built rapport quickly, and I thought she would make a great addition to the team. Similar in age to me, she had plenty of experience and I knew she would work well with many of the customers we had in the Northeast and Canada. Bill and his peers weren't comfortable hiring her. I was asked to consider hiring internally versus externally as there were Mid-Market New Business reps who were unhappy in their role and wanted to try Customer Growth as a better fit.

WTF? Is my team the stop where New Business reps go to find their place in the world when they can't cut it in their current role? The lack of respect our Customer Growth teams received was unbelievable. We brought in more revenue than individual New Business teams, but we were always treated like the ugly stepchildren in the sales organization. I had witnessed the difference in respect firsthand when I was a sales rep on the founding Customer Growth team, but now I had a front-row seat witnessing it as a Customer Growth sales leader. Since our Customer Growth team reported into New Business executive sales leaders, we always played second fiddle to New Business thought processes and decision-making.

Bill and his superiors asked me to "respectfully consider hiring within vs. moving forward with the external candidate." I couldn't help but laugh inside. Not the funny, ha-ha kind of laugh, but the frustrated kind of laugh. When I tried to hire internally with top-performing Kristen, all hell broke loose, but I guess it's OK to palm off poor performers from New Business on my team with no concern for my opinion on the candidate's ability to do the job.

Red Flag #1

Glaring Red Flag
I followed my sales leader's "recommendation" and welcomed this New Business rep to my team on December 1, 2022. He didn't even last until the end of March 2023. He wasn't happy about the company not adjusting his base salary when he moved from New Business to Customer Growth.

Sorry, Buddy. Join the club. (I didn't get a raise either when I made the move between teams two years before, and I was a top performer). It turns out he had been interviewing externally before I even hired him. He accepted a position with one of our competitors. This meant I had yet another open head count to fill on my team.

Back to the hiring board. I interviewed candidate after candidate. This time, I had the support to hire externally, and another female account executive impressed me. She had limited software sales experience, but after several rounds of interviews introducing her to Kristen and Bill, her fun, positive attitude and charismatic personality won us over. Give me a positive attitude and genuine effort all day long. I can teach the necessary skills to ramp up quickly on sales acumen or educate on product knowledge with our software solutions. She had it all, but the sales leadership above Bill was hung up on her limited software experience. She didn't come from our competitors or have years of selling software in her DNA. I didn't care. She had the charisma and personality I was looking for to build long-term relationships within our customer base, and I knew she would be a great addition to my team.

Again, I was asked to consider other candidates. Male candidates. A guy who had software experience from all the right companies but when I hired him couldn't put a sentence together in an email without coming across as a smarmy con man. He apparently interviewed well for a New Business role, but because there weren't any openings in either Corporate or Mid-Market on the East Coast, he was "highly recommended for me to hire in Customer Growth."

Red Flag #2

Glaring Red Flag
He started in mid-February 2023 during our sales kickoff in Orlando and didn't make it past ninety days before we released him to his future.

Around this same time, several top performing sales reps had reached out to me and Bill to learn more about our open head count. Several of them were in the Corporate segment rolling up to Annie and her manager. It was a natural career progression for them to move up market rather than stay in Corporate to continue their sales career. I had started mentoring one of the female sales reps after an introduction from Kristen just a few months prior. She was interested in moving to Mid-Market and asked her leader's permission to speak with Bill and me. We both had calls with her and answered her questions.

Denial—Top Performers Don't Get Laid Off

It wasn't a big deal.

Until it was.

Knowing the shit-show Bill and I dealt with Kristen's promotion, we were very careful not to make any promises within the sales organization without the seal of approval from Gordon. To ensure we didn't face this wrath again, Bill sent me a screenshot of a text message with Gordon. It was a directive for him (and me) to make sure we don't talk to anyone in the sales organization about our open roles until we get permission from their incumbent sales leader.

Reading this text chain made my blood boil. Are we all back in high school again where you can't talk to certain people, otherwise you'll get beat up? Literally and figuratively, this is what it felt like—reverting to high school with the you-can't-talk-to-him-or-her games.

"We can't win," Bill said. "Moving forward, I guess we need approval to talk to anyone."

"NOTHING HAPPENED!" I exclaimed.

"We took a call. Guess that's no good," he explained.

I was really ticked off. What Gordon failed to recognize in his directive was that her sales leader gave permission weeks ago. He forgot.

"I know. Trust me. I was like, WTF," Bill said.

"Annie's boss told her it was fine to reach out. Now, we are getting in trouble again?" I questioned. I was so sick and tired of this corporate bullshit. "This is not even remotely close to the Kristen situation, so they need to let that go. Maybe people see we have a good thing going on in Mid-Market Customer Growth. Maybe the Corporate team needs to get their house in order so that so many people won't be so eager to jump ship and leave."

The Layoff Cooties – It's Them, Not You

I was livid.

My name was being dragged through the mud with sales leadership (again), and I didn't do anything wrong other than answer questions about my team to a colleague.

Bill explained this to me like he was a good little soldier, obeying the chain of command: "It's the new rule after Kristen. People need to be here at least a full year if not two to progress through. Same for people moving from our team if they want to go to Enterprise. It helps prevent rogue movements and gets everyone off our back about 'poaching.'"

The truth is, our company put none of these promotion rules in writing. Management made it up as they went along so their rules would apply to the politics of the sales organization's current patriarchal bureaucracy. Sales leadership thought they were being smart with how this was being communicated, but with no written policy in place, everyone knew sales leadership made organizational changes to benefit them. Sales leadership formed their opinions on where everyone should fit into their sales picture. Damn *you* if you attempted to move that puzzle piece before *they* were ready.

Amid the internal politicking, my team was doing our job and closing (winning) business on the East Coast. Bill led the West Coast sales reps, but he was having difficulty forecasting deals and getting them over the line to signature. My East Coast team was pulling the weight of the entire Mid-Market Customer Growth team, and I was accomplishing it with fewer people in seats. If I could get my open head count hired to full strength and ramped up quickly, there was no reason we couldn't finish the year strong.

Every spring, our company hosted a huge annual event in Las Vegas, Nevada, where thousands of our customers and select prospects gathered for a week to learn about our exciting new software offerings. It's one big party with sessions during the workday to help sober up before the drink-fest continues at the evening's happy hour and into the night. Our Customer Growth team was mostly in attendance with a few sales folks from New Business who were allowed to go because their prospects were going to be there. To keep costs low for internal attendees, sales reps needed a specific number of customers or prospects attending from their territory. We usually didn't have any problems getting our customers to attend, so our Customer Growth team was there in full force.

Justin was one of the New Business sales leaders who qualified to go based on his pipeline and prospects in attendance. He and I met up a few times throughout the week in between sessions. He told me there was a list being circulated that very week with people's names on it who were being laid off. It would affect a lot of our North American sales teams on the New Business side of the organization. He was freaking out, not knowing if his name would be on the list, because he was a relatively new sales leader.

Everyone in sales could tell there was a different vibe compared to previous years at this event. The week in Vegas commenced, and as the saying goes, "What happens in Vegas, stays in Vegas."

Except that's not what happened.

Shortly after the Vegas meeting, our company received the news in early May that our beloved CEO made the impromptu decision to leave earlier than expected. He was supposed to stay for the first year of transition from public to private company. Gordon held a leadership call with his direct and indirect reports, including me. He communicated the CEO update and asked for us to focus on long-term goals, to bring in more business, and to control what we could control as leaders. Gordon said this was an example of situational leadership and that each of us would remember this moment, the way we reacted, and how we led our teams through adversity. He asked us to meet with the top talent on our teams and over communicate. There would be a press release going out shortly, naming the interim CEO.

I shared the news with my team, copying Gordon and Bill on my email. I also gave my team the opportunity to share their feelings on a team call. I strived to provide a psychologically safe environment for them to operate in, just like I would want to have if I were in their shoes. My email ended with, "As each of YOU are top talent in this sales organization, please let me know how I can help, even if it's just to vent your concerns. Talk soon."

Kristen messaged back: "You're the best, Laura. You are also top talent."

"Yes, thank you for letting us know! And agree 10000% with Kristen," another responded.

Our CEO's sudden departure in early May put a temporary halt on the pending layoff rumors and that infamous list being circulated around the sales organization. Apparently, May was the scheduled time for the layoffs to begin, but with our CEO's surprising news, the company delayed the inevitable layoffs another month as the interim leadership team tried to quell the tension.

Stories of people's names being on a spreadsheet one week and then removed the next week permeated through the three sales segments of Corporate, Mid-Market, and Enterprise.

It was now mid-May 2023 and the idea of Kristen being hand picked to lead the West Coast team was also dropped in my lap as an additional stressor to the layoff rumors. I knew our Customer Growth team wouldn't lose people with the layoffs. We didn't have enough head count on my team to support the customers on the East Coast. So, if anything, I would gain team members. And that's exactly what happened.

On June 1, 2023, Bill called with the names of five sales reps who were being moved from New Business to Customer Growth, effective immediately. We had no control over who they were; in fact, Bill and I barely recognized some names. I was told to call each of them as soon as possible, welcome them to our team, and say that we were excited to have them on Customer Growth. There was no time to hem and haw over the decisions that were made on our behalf, but we could guarantee that Gordon had his hand in determining who would be on our team.

Bill sent me everyone's cell phone number, and I dialed each one. I had the same conversation with all five New Business sales reps. I welcomed them to the Customer Growth team and asked them to be prepared for our first one-on-one the following Monday with answers to these four questions:

1. What are your expectations of yourself in this new role?
2. What are your expectations of your teammates?
3. What are your expectations of me as your sales leader?
4. What are you going to do when things don't go your way?

It was extremely important for me to set the tone and culture immediately with these new folks. I called out the elephant in the room in each conversation, telling each one

The Layoff Cooties – It's Them, Not You

this is a new development for all of us, and we have two choices: we can come together or we can fall apart as a team and face the same fate as colleagues laid off that same day.

I had my work cut out for me. Overnight, I went from a team of two to a team of seven. I was determined to make my team successful, but we had to get on the same page. The direction of a sales team is directly proportional to the leadership at its helm. This was my moment to show what we could achieve despite the adversity in our way. We would continue being a top-performing team.

Top performers don't get laid off.

There's no denying it.

They do.

6   Anger—This Is Not Who I Want to Be

If I had to choose one grief stage that triggered the most visceral feelings throughout the days and weeks after my layoff, it would be anger. But who am I as a person if I remain angry for an extended period of time? I had to deal with my anger constructively, in a way that was both healing and representative of who I was as a person. First, I needed to validate those feelings of anger by creating a list. Why was I so angry in the first place?

I was angry because I know I was one of my company's top leaders.

I was angry because I know I didn't deserve this after everything I had achieved.

I was angry because I know this was a calculated decision that had nothing to do with my name being on a spreadsheet to improve the bottom line.

I was angry because … this was personal.

I continuously replayed the events of my last two months of employment prior to getting that November 29, 2023 email saying, "Your Role Is Impacted." I couldn't shake the feeling that something specific triggered my name being put on a layoff list. A list that didn't include any other sales leaders but me at a company that employed over two thousand people globally.

As I replayed the weeks and months leading up, all I could find was probable cause.

The probable cause was that I was the thorn in their side they wanted to remove.

These events seemed hardly coincidental. So, let's backtrack a little …

Early October 2023
I received a call from Bill telling me two sales reps on my team would get an immediate salary increase. It was a way to incentivize top performers, or executive leadership's perception of the top performers, from potentially leaving the company. There were a lot of changes in the sales organization since the PE takeover and executive leadership wanted to keep top performers and anyone at risk of leaving from looking elsewhere. No one ever asked my opinion on who should get this adjustment on my team. Instead, two sales reps received increases in their base pay that separated my salary and theirs by only $5k.

I was shocked. I was insulted. I was, you guessed it, angry.

I was leading an entire team of sales professionals through a challenging internal and external climate with an unachievable team quota and these two sales reps who were not even performing well year-to-date automatically received $20K and $25K increases in salary, respectively?

You have got to be kidding me.

Bill instructed me to call both of them to share the good news. My immediate reaction was to tell Bill to call them himself because I had nothing to do with this ridiculous decision. In my opinion, neither of them warranted the increase based on their performance, and it infuriated me that I was only making a few thousand dollars more than them in salary now. Politically, I knew there was nothing I could do to change executive management's mind on these salary bumps. I wasn't even consulted prior to the decision being made. This was clearly an out-of-annual-cycle adjustment. Why was this allowed for them, but not for me? I followed Bill's directives because there was nothing I could do at that point. Politics above my pay grade made this decision to adjust my sales rep's salaries. I didn't have any other choice. Bill wouldn't communicate the news. I had to do it.

    I called both sales reps to share their good fortune. Their excitement was very short-lived. One rep already was working on leaving our company, and used the increase to negotiate an even higher salary with a competitor. That rep was gone less than two weeks later. The other sales rep wound up leaving our company voluntarily a few months after my layoff.

    Great job, executive leadership … the incentive to keep two perceived top sales reps at the company backfired. I'm sure both left laughing all the way to the bank, not letting the door hit them from behind.

Friday, November 3, 2023
I had a regularly scheduled one-on-one with Annie on a Friday morning. She knew I wasn't happy about the salary increases that were doled out to my team and my own grievances about not being paid fairly dating back to when I was first hired.

    She advised me to respect the hierarchy and have a conversation with Bill to let him "fight the good fight" on my behalf. She also instructed me to put together a thoughtful breakdown of my contributions over the years and have everything in writing for him to plead my case. Then she reiterated how Gordon hates when people talk about salaries among the teams. I couldn't help but think: *of course he does—he knows the company pays everyone differently, and the company pays men more than women.* Everyone in the sales organization knew this because sales reps shared their compensation plans with one another. As a leader, I also had access to salary information. All the women on my team earned less than the men, and that was just a small cross section.

Annie would tell me she never had much luck fighting for her salary increases over the years. Ironically, it was almost like she wore it as a badge of honor. As if it was something she was willing to deal with because "that's just how it is." An aw-shucks mentality. Like we should just be grateful we have a freaking job there.

Annie was one of the few women who assimilated with the bro culture at the company. She was considered "one of the guys," although I always thought it was often at her own expense. The patriarchal sales leaders constantly were using her as an example to poke fun at something she did. Whether it was work-related or personal, the joke always came back to Annie laughing it off in a meeting. I guess if you can't beat 'em, join 'em?

Yet, I still respected her counsel and took action.

I sent Bill a Slack message later that afternoon asking to chat on Monday. I was not feeling valued at the company anymore, and I told him so. He wanted to call me right away, but my weekend was just beginning on the East Coast while he was still working on the West Coast. Plus, I knew

Anger—This is Not Who I Want to Be

I needed to prepare my thoughts for our discussion. I told him it could wait until Monday.

Monday, November 6th
On Monday morning, I sent the following email to Bill.

> In preparation for our 1:1 today, I'm including some talking points to guide our discussion:
>
> - Gordon shared on a leadership call not too long ago that he would appreciate his team reaching out if we felt there was an opportunity to advance our career elsewhere vs. part of his leadership team.
>
> - My preference is to continue building out the Customer Growth team but I do not feel my overall compensation package is commensurate with my consistent performance and 24+ years of sales experience.
>
> As such, I am asking for a salary adjustment of $20K effective 12/1 and 2024 sponsorship of my Chief membership. With the most recent sales rep salary adjustment made to keep high performing reps, there is only a $5K difference in salary compared to my base. I am asking for your support to propose an increase in salary before the end of 2023.
>
> I thought: *if the company could make salary adjustments out-of-cycle for my sales reps, then why couldn't I receive one as*

well? It was important to be direct and let him know exactly what I was negotiating so Bill could go to bat for me.

Chief is a private membership network of about twenty thousand executive and C-suite women that I joined after I became a regional vice president of sales in 2022. At the time I joined, each Chief member was placed in a core group with five to six other highly successful female leaders. There is an executive coach facilitating the monthly sessions, supporting one another on a peer advisory journey and leadership program throughout the year. Today, there are several membership programs, but when I joined, Chief charged an annual fee of $5k–$7k. I paid for this membership out of pocket as an investment in myself toward being a better leader.

Many women in Chief are sponsored by their companies. I had asked once before to get this reimbursed and sales management denied me. Now I was asking again as my membership fee was up for renewal in January. My company didn't offer any leadership training like this. I felt it was an important part of my professional development toward being a better leader.

In the rest of the email to Bill, I tied my achievements back to the company's three core values highlighting the millions of dollars in sales I brought in, the 123 percent and 155 percent to annual quota achievements as a founding member of the Customer Growth team, and my stellar four- and five-star performance reviews as a top-performing sales professional. I highlighted my strong communication skills with a focus on conflict resolution, collaboration with customers and internal stakeholders, finding solutions and problem solving. I described the strategic account plans

Anger—This is Not Who I Want to Be

I created that allowed my team to manage hundreds of customers, thus impacting tens of millions of dollars to the company's bottom line.

I provided examples of my impact as a proactive and positive change agent, often proposing new ideas that simplified processes seamlessly with other departments to improve and eliminate internal red tape. Finally, I highlighted how my mentorship and training of countless sales reps helped so many of them become top performers across market segments in their own right.

I knew my worth.

I knew what other sales leaders made. Male and female.

I knew what I was getting paid compared to my sales reps.

I was simply asking to be made whole.

I went on with the rest of my morning, not giving much thought to the email I sent Bill. We always had a very open communication style with one another. We didn't hold anything back in our relationship whether it was personal or professional. We both knew each other's families; we sent food porn pictures of our favorite meals; we texted and Slacked regularly, even on the weekends and all hours of the night. There was absolutely no reason for me to be worried or nervous about having this important conversation with him later that day.

I could tell as soon as I jumped on the Zoom that Monday afternoon with Bill, his demeanor was different.

Looking back on this moment, this was probably my first strike.

He didn't ask about my weekend. He was not interested in any small talk like usual. He did not appear to be in a good mood at all. I was not prepared for the things he was

The Layoff Cooties – It's Them, Not You

about to say to me. It was so out of character and quite frankly, shocking.

He first asked me if our call was being recorded.

WTF, seriously?

"Of course not." I replied.

He asked me if someone else wrote my email for me, as in someone at Chief.

OMG, I can write my own damn emails, thank you.

"Of course not." I replied again.

He then proceeded to tell me that my email felt like a demand letter, and that I was always complaining about my salary.

OUCH.

That one cut like a knife through my soul.

Bill was one of the first people I met at this company. We were close enough that he knew my salary history grievances over the years and being passed over for increases as a top-performing sales rep. When he became my leader, he promised to help correct that as best he could. When the company promoted me into sales leadership, he fought for me to be paid fairly. At the time of my promotion into leadership, I felt like I was made whole. Once I started learning male sales leaders with less experience and poorer sales results earned more, and sales reps on my team were getting salary increases up to $5K less than what I was earning, I had to speak up.

I couldn't believe what I was hearing. I'm not the type of person who is ever speechless, but at that moment, the tone and manner in which Bill was speaking stunned me. There was such a lack of respect by asking me if I was recording the call, and if someone wrote my email for me. He knew

Anger—This is Not Who I Want to Be

me better than that. I could fight my own battles, which is what I was doing by initiating the conversation about my compensation.

As prepared as I felt for this important discussion, a million thoughts were going through my head. I eventually gained my composure and confidence back in the next few seconds, telling him I didn't think it was a demand letter at all, and I was sorry if he thought it came across that way.

Wait, why the hell am I apologizing?

Given my history regarding my pay, coupled with knowing male leaders earned more, and then seeing my sales team given salary adjustments within reach of my pay, it didn't make any sense why Bill was turning this into something I should be ashamed of asking to be fixed.

Bill gave me some options on how we could proceed. Clearly, the time between when I sent my email and our meeting, he had given this a lot of thought. I wondered if he talked with Annie or Gordon about it before our call that afternoon. Bill was not a traditional sales leader, meaning he didn't climb the corporate ladder as a sales rep prior to leading a sales team. His tenure at our company was working with customers in a support role prior to being selected to lead our Customer Growth sales team. He leaned on Annie a lot for sales advice and management protocol. Many people used to joke about how he followed Annie around like a little lost puppy dog at sales meetings. Infatuation comes in many forms, and it was obvious he respected her sales acumen and counsel.

Bill didn't think the timing was right to bring up salary grievances, given that it was nearing the end of the year. Holidays were right around the corner; annual performance review time and focal reviews would be here before we knew it; he thought I should wait until a later point when he could go to bat for me again. But when? I couldn't wait for management to just bump my salary up like they did for my sales reps.

Mr. Politician was once again trying to control the narrative.

He didn't want to go to bat for me. Lately, he didn't want to do anything that would rock the boat. And asking for an out-of-cycle pay raise for me was a huge rocking of the boat.

I felt like this was an excuse.

I saw his request to hold off as a deliberate failure on his part to do what was right for a leader on his team. I was one of his top performers. Bill did well when I did well. He would often tell me he'd be lost without my leadership on the team. It was in his best interests to keep me happy and content to keep building our sales pipeline, leading my team effectively through significant change, and closing millions of dollars of business as I had done for years.

To say that I was very upset after my call with him would be an understatement.

I shared with Kristen what happened on my call with Bill. I also updated her on what Annie had instructed me to do the Friday before, so she knew I was following her directive.

Kristen expressed surprise at how Bill handled my one-on-one and the news that Annie had given me to never bring up salary grievances with Gordon. Kristen knew about the salary adjustments my sales reps received on my team. I told her I wouldn't think about my conversation with Bill anymore.

Kristen was still very green where corporate politics and difficult conversations transpired. But she was smart enough to realize it didn't make much sense either. It was really important she knew everything that was going on behind the scenes. Our relationship was built on trust and loyalty to one another. I was confident that would never change between us.

Tuesday, November 7, 2023
The next day, I focused on getting more answers about backfilling the open roles on my team. Ideally, I'd get my open seats filled before the end of the year so any ramping and training could begin before the start of a new fiscal year in February. With the change in PE ownership, our sales and fiscal year shifted, ending in January instead of December. This benefited our sales organization this year because we now had thirteen months to hit our annual quotas versus just twelve.

December and January were shaping up to be big months for us to close out the fiscal year. Our company held our annual Sales Kick Off (SKO) meeting in Florida every February too. SKOs bring together the entire global sales organization in one place to set the stage for a successful fiscal year ahead. Many training and team-building events happen there, and I wanted to ensure my team was in full strength in preparation to hit the ground running next year.

Annie's Corporate Customer Growth team had two leaders for the East and West, like our structure in Mid-Market. I learned one of the open positions on her West Coast leader's team the sales leadership filled internally when a New Business sales rep moved to Customer Growth in the previous week.

"Why is Annie's team actively still interviewing for her backfill? She is speaking with one of my mentees tomorrow and another rep just got moved over to her team. I'm curious why this is allowed, but I don't have the green light for my backfill?" I asked Bill.

"Annie got hers approved before the freeze. Internal transfers are OK, I guess. I don't know what I'm supposed to say anymore on this topic, Laura. I am asking weekly," he said.

"I don't know either, but there always seems to be a reason why things are allowed for other people but not for me. I will do what I can with what I can. It's my job to ask questions. So thanks for answering." I said in a passive aggressive way.

He must have sensed my frustration and anger, so he continued to prod.

"Guess I'm not sure what this is related to," he said.

"I'm just telling you, this doesn't make any sense," I replied.

"The hiring freeze doesn't impact internal transfers. Guess that's the point here," he offered up.

Wow—this was news to me—and seemed to change by the day.

"So I can hire someone ASAP, if it's agreed upon internally?" I questioned.

"ASAP is relative, as is everything right now, but my understanding is yes."

This still didn't make any sense.

I had a short list of folks internally I know would have jumped immediately to be on my team from their current roles. If this was an allowable option under the supposed hiring freeze, then why couldn't we have conversations with folks internally and get them moved into my open head count? Check that ... why couldn't *I* have conversations with folks internally? Clearly, Annie's team could proceed. I grew increasingly angry at this travesty.

Again, I shared this news with Kristen. She didn't have any immediate open positions on her team, but she wanted to make some personnel changes over the next few months. She was always open to having conversations with folks internally and externally to scope out potential hires.

I Slacked the HR representative assigned to our sales team asking him to help me understand what the policy was to backfill open positions. I explained the situation from Annie's team. No response from HR.

Wednesday, November 8th, 2023
The next day, I Slacked HR again, asking the same question and reiterating how I expected an answer. He immediately responded and said he was trying to get in touch with his boss to find out for me. Hmm ... shouldn't he know the policy on hiring for the sales organization as our main contact? Classic, politically correct response from a buttoned-up HR professional.

My hands were tied.

Later that day, Bill responded to the email I sent him before our heated one-on-one on Monday. As soon as I read through his response, I immediately thought, *this is far too formal of a response from him.* I didn't think anyone else wrote his email for him like he accused me of doing, but I did find his formal wording representative of other emails he had written when he wanted to document something with another party, like HR. It read:

> Thank you for bringing the below back to my attention and walking me through your needs heading into End of Year/Focal Reviews. After a day of reflection, I wanted to recap a few of our key points and action items:

- Your results have, and continue to, speak for themselves. I have faith in your ability to coach, manage, and create a culture of productivity within your team. Today we discussed compensation, but if you feel my support in other areas isn't sufficient, I'd enjoy the opportunity to discuss that in our next 1:1 to find ways to support you more effectively.

When looking at our three core values, I agree that you have always put forth your best effort in all areas. However, please always balance your side projects, data analytics, etc. with activities that will directly impact your current team and yourself. I say this only because I do not want you to get "burnt out" by trying to do too much at once. Focus on the controllables, continue to be the dedicated coach you are to your team that they respect and love, and the rest will play out like it's supposed to. This should help continue to aid in the healthy work/life balance that we all strive for.

- Our agreed follow up from this call was for you to digest our conversation, and then let me know how you'd prefer to proceed from here. Our options include 1) working together to re-draft an email stating your justification for a mid-year adjustment. I will take the conversation to Gordon personally, then have you send him your justification directly following that meeting. 2) You take the conversation to Gordon directly. I would follow your lead on how you'd like to handle this, if you'd like me involved, etc. or 3) We finish out Q4, put together a strong focal review and look to see what adjustments can be made into 2024.

I write this email as a respectful push, in partnership with you, with the hope that we can put compensation discussions behind us. Since our time together in this structure, it's been a recurring conversation. You, nor I, should be spending stress-inducing hours worrying about compensation multiple times per year. We provide so much opportunity and value to these teams, and that should be our pride/focus on a monthly/quarterly basis and my genuine hope is that you'll trust that, when I'm able to, I'll have your back.

Wow!
Where do I even begin to tear apart this BS corporate response?
I was angry.
No. Angry is an understatement.
I was furious.
This was corporate speak, and I couldn't help but feel like HR was probably blind-copied on this email. Bill had a history of bcc'ing me and Kristen on important emails that went up the food chain, so there was no reason to believe he wouldn't do the same in this scenario to protect himself with HR. In retrospect, there was a lot of bcc'ing at our company, so what does that really say about working in a

trusting corporate environment? Not much, apparently. A lot of CYA (Cover Your Ass) behavior was fairly commonplace. Regardless, he had never communicated like this with me in such a formal way in one-on-one email correspondence; reading through his bulleted responses over and over again angered me even more.

They were cop-outs.

Excuses.

Opportunities for him to pass the buck back to me without dirtying his hands.

My *least favorite* part?

> "I write this email as a respectful push, in partnership with you, with the hope that we can put compensation discussions behind us. Since our time together in this structure, it's been a recurring conversation."

I felt like screaming from the top of my lungs, *"It's been a recurring conversation because fair pay has ALWAYS been a problem!"*

My second *least favorite* part?

> "Please always balance your side projects, data analytics, etc. with activities that will directly impact your current team and yourself. I say this only because I do not want you to get 'burnt out' by trying to do too much at once."

I didn't have a history of burnout, nor did I ever complain about having too many side projects or activities. I

Anger—This is Not Who I Want to Be

kept up with my work load just fine and often made time to help others complete their responsibilities as well. Sales Operations and other internal teams often solicited me to help provide sales insights and recommendations on how to improve sales reporting, revamping the customer referral process with marketing, and helping to lead initiatives within our female-focused, company-wide empowered teams.

Why was he telling me to focus on my team only and control "the controllables"?

I no longer had an ally in Bill.

If I wanted to get answers on my salary grievances, pay inequity issues between men and women in the sales organization, backfilling head count on my team, or anything else requiring executive approval, I needed to take matters into my own hands. Bill made it very clear from this communication, and over the previous few months, that he didn't want to rattle any cages. Shortly after the PE takeover, Bill often shared he wanted to manage from the sidelines and not highlight any of our issues that would bring attention to our team. I disagreed with this philosophy and believed the best chance we had for change was to speak up.

Bill knew I was upset about the open head count issue and not being able to backfill my open roles immediately. What he didn't know at that time was that I went directly to Gordon's immediate boss, Jack Watkins, to get answers. Jack and I had developed a one-on-one cadence that both Bill and Gordon were unaware of happening. Knowing I didn't have an ally with Bill or Gordon, I decided to go straight to the top of the food chain.

Jack was relatively new to the company, having been there for less than six months. He began as a consultant with the

The Layoff Cooties – It's Them, Not You

PE firm who purchased our company, but eventually accepted a chief commercial officer role, supporting the entire global sales organization. Gordon was one of his direct reports. Jack had a new energy about him. He was transparent and friendly. He did not manage based on closed conversations or fear-based directives. I had a good rapport with him after introducing myself directly when he was first hired.

We emailed regularly, and I shared positive updates about my sales team. I wanted him to know the good things my team was achieving together. Jack was always responsive, usually communicating back by email within the same day, and complimenting my team for our monthly successes. Before Jack, executive sales leadership didn't celebrate sales wins with much excitement. Automatically generated, company-wide sales notifications would be emailed when a deal moved to "Closed-Won" in our Salesforce CRM, but it was very much a "what have you done for me lately" sales organization. In other words, *great job on closing that deal; now go and win more.*

Wednesday, November 15th, 2023
I drafted an email to Jack inquiring about my open head count, but I called Kristen before pushing SEND. I read her the message and asked her opinion. She agreed that I should send it, especially since we both saw our colleagues were posting job listings on LinkedIn that very week to backfill roles on their New Business teams. My email to Jack informed him I had many customers who were not getting the attention they deserve because I wasn't able to backfill my open roles. I didn't want to introduce an interim sales rep because many of our customers had already seen too many sales rep changes in the last few months since the June sales

reorganization. I stated this was very important to me and that I didn't feel like I was being heard. Looking back, this was probably strike number two.

Thursday, November 16th, 2023
Jack emailed me back the next afternoon:

> Hi Laura – sorry for the delay, hectic morning. I am working with the leadership team on a holistic global list of priorities for backfill and balancing against the budget for next year. We are going to hire both New Business and Customer Growth teams. Give me a week or so and we should have clarity on available/open head count we can fill. Gordon was on my team meeting this AM and shared the global need for the Mid-Market and Corporate segments. Have a nice weekend.

There you have it.
Our sales teams were continuing to grow.
More hiring would be happening.
I felt better about the timeline because he said he'd know more in the next week. I was happy and content with that response. It was better than the vacillating back-and-forth responses I was getting for the last few weeks. I still didn't know if I could hire internally or externally, but it didn't matter. I heard from the man at the top of the food chain directly.

Friday, November 17th, 2023
I was on PTO celebrating an early birthday weekend. I always take off work for my November 20th birthday. This year it

fell on a Monday, so I took off both Friday and Monday to make it a long weekend. I had scheduled dentist appointments for myself and Kelsie that Friday anyway, so no need to try to work in between running around town. On Friday afternoon, around lunchtime, I got a text message from Bill:

> Did you reach out to Jack directly about head count?

Jack must have mentioned my outreach to Gordon in their executive leadership meeting, and now Gordon was asking Bill to confirm if this was done.

I was in the car driving with Kelsie to our dentist appointment.

I called Kristen in a panic. She was at the airport waiting to board a flight. I didn't know how to respond to Bill's text. Part of me wanted to reply with a *HELL, YEAH I DID* type of response, but Kristen calmed me down and suggested a more simple and diplomatic response.

I texted Bill back with a short and simple reply:

> Yes.

Bill gave it a thumbs-up acknowledgment.

I knew this was not good news. He was respecting the fact that I was on PTO, but I sensed he was dying to call me and chew me out for disrespecting the leadership hierarchy. Going above Bill to Gordon was one thing. But going above Gordon to Jack? Whoa, that was a whole new level of ballsiness.

I had a busy birthday weekend ahead, and I would not let this ruin it.

Tuesday, November 21st, 2023
I flew to Canada for the Thanksgiving holiday at my sister's house that Tuesday morning after my birthday PTO commenced and was back on the clock for work. I had a bunch of calls I was taking from the airport earlier in the morning and then later at my sister's house that day. Bill wanted to catch up in the afternoon. We didn't have time to chat until later that evening. I didn't mind; it was after hours because there were a few customer issues I needed to bring to his attention. Sales life is 24/7. When you need to get stuff done, it doesn't matter the hour. You just do it.

Before I could get into anything related to my customers, Bill started off by telling me I caused a lot of problems by reaching out to Jack about head count. Both he and Gordon were pretty pissed off. Even though it was a phone call, I could visualize Bill sitting in his home office laying into me.

My heart was racing, but I confidently fought back.

"I don't think I did anything wrong, Bill. I wasn't getting the answers I needed from you, Gordon or HR. Interestingly enough, Jack was able to answer my questions to my satisfaction," I said.

"You shouldn't have done that. I gave you all the information I had at the time," he responded.

We went back and forth for the next twenty minutes.

He thought I was out of line.

I didn't think I was.

The discussion from our one-on-one, and my asking for a pay increase had transpired two weeks prior, so there was

The Layoff Cooties – It's Them, Not You

a lot of underlying friction felt during that phone call. It had been building up. Even though we didn't discuss that topic specifically, my bringing up these issues to our sales leaders against his recommendation agitated him. I didn't care. The company gave me a job to do, and I didn't have a full team in place to even come close to meeting those expectations. I was fighting an uphill battle. I didn't think my boss would ever fight against me. I'm not the type of person to sit by the wayside and let things happen. I'm a mover and a shaker. I want to be part of finding solutions to problems. Why did they ask me to move into leadership if they didn't want me to fight for these things? If they were looking for a YES woman who only followed orders, that was not me. They should have known better.

My sister overheard the entire conversation. When I got off, she said, "Wow, that was pretty heated. Is everything OK?"

"Yeah, my boss just didn't like that I went over his head to try and get answers about something. It will blow over when I get back next week after Thanksgiving. I'm not going to worry about it anymore. Let's plan our Thanksgiving feast!"

Aside from calling Kristen and filling her in with the details of my conversation with Bill, I didn't give it any more thought the rest of the week. Kristen, Bill and I had a fun call the next day with our entire Mid-Market Customer Growth team as we headed into the Thanksgiving holiday.

It wasn't until after my layoff that I put the pieces together.

I believe going above Gordon's head was the final strike that put me on the layoff list.

Gordon sat in a position of power and had complete control of who was on these lists from previous rounds of layoffs. After years of my speaking up about pay inequity as a rep and as a leader, after the political nonsense and drama related to Kristen being promoted to my team and accusations of trying to poach her and other reps, and after going above Gordon's head to Jack to get answers on head count for my team, I was now being silenced.

The ultimate silence.

The "Your Role Is Impacted" kind of silence.

Now, can you see why I was so angry?

Monday, December 4th, 2023 (Five days after my layoff)

My anger increased in the immediate days after my layoff. Unable to get personal information from my laptop before the company shut down my network access, I wanted the motivational emails and professional development materials I had created as a leader.

I invested heavily in providing personal and professional development training for my entire Customer Growth sales team and the women I mentored. These were not company-specific materials. No corporate dollars were used to create the resources for my team. I would share video links of TED Talks for them to watch, and we'd discuss them as a group. I'd read a Brené Brown book, summarize it, and then lead with an insightful discussion on our weekly team calls. I'd send motivational emails to my team regularly to keep them in good spirits. It's extremely important for sales professionals to maintain a positive attitude because rejection is associated with the role. The ups and downs of sales represent the craziest ride mentally, emotionally, and professionally. I had so many materials I created from scratch I wanted back.

The Layoff Cooties – It's Them, Not You

I texted the four guys on my team, Kristen, and another mentee, asking them to send me some of those professional development files and emails. I also wanted a copy of the #FridayFunFacts team-building Google Sheet I created earlier in the year that had their weekly responses to questions. Every week, I would send them five questions to answer to get to know one another. I wanted a copy of their answers for the year as a keepsake. These weren't confidential documents. They were personal and professional development materials I curated that had nothing to do with our company's insignia or confidential intelligent property information.

Well, one or more of those six people that I trusted implicitly went to HR and said I was asking for confidential company information. I quickly received a letter from HR to my personal email with the following directive: "You have reached out to several employees asking for work products, such as presentation materials ... the materials you asked for are company property. Please cease from asking for materials/documents from our employees." The letter also asked me to remove a LinkedIn post where I had named customers. It was a gratitude post thanking about forty of my favorite customers in the days after my layoff. I was simply sharing publicly that I greatly appreciated our four years of working together. My former employer thought their competitors could use this to harm their business.

Guess what, Einsteins? Your competitors already know who your customers are, as they can buy lists from many sources to get that information. Your competitors can also pick up the phone and often find out through their own sales evaluations who the incumbent provider is for any kind of software. I highly doubt my little LinkedIn post of gratitude reaching less than one millionth of a percentage of the one billion people on LinkedIn was going to take down your business overnight. C'mon people. Grow the F-up.

I wasn't sharing anything that wasn't already publicly available. I was thanking my customers for their support, transparency, and our time working together, which I greatly appreciated. How is what I did any different from my former company posting customer logos and customer reviews on their website? That also lets competition know who their customers are, doesn't it? Who knew you could get reprimanded for showing gratitude? I seriously don't know what this world is coming to sometimes!

The letter from HR continued to state if I didn't remove or revise the LinkedIn post, then I would no longer be eligible for my severance package.

Holy shit. This was getting out of hand and completely blown out of proportion.

I immediately pulled up my LinkedIn account, took a screenshot of the post in question and comments received to date, and deleted the entire gratitude post. It wasn't worth this ridiculous drama my former employer was creating. I emailed HR right away to let them know their request was now complete.

I was still furious thinking about which of those six people threw me under the bus and purposefully went to HR. After *everything* I had done for each of them over the years since we met, and this is how they pay me back? What made one or more of them go to HR? Were they bullied by sales leadership, asking if any of them heard from me? Did they seriously think I was a threat? I mean, come on! I was the one whose livelihood was taken away disrespectfully. Not theirs. I cared about them as friends and human beings. At least I thought they knew that.

I later found out through multiple sources that Annie instructed both Corporate and Mid-Market Customer Growth teams to stop communicating with me. If any of them sent me anything, their jobs would be in jeopardy. She said sales leadership was monitoring their emails accordingly. Many of the folks on my team took this to an extreme level, disconnecting and/or blocking me on LinkedIn. Did I have layoff cooties? Did they think they would be next in a layoff simply by being connected on LinkedIn or keeping in touch as friends?

It all hurt so much.

My heart ached emotionally.

My entire body physically felt the pain.

But I knew I couldn't be angry forever.

That is not who I wanted to be.

I didn't realize at the time how hurtful the appearance of disconnecting from me on a social media platform would make me feel. For some of my former work colleagues, I didn't see their disconnection for weeks. They weren't daily posters on LinkedIn, so it's not like I was missing anything from the feed. I noticed it more when I would see their names popping up on other people's posts in the comments section. Now instead of first connections, they were second connections, so they must have unfollowed me deliberately. It made me wonder what kind of negative narrative was happening within the walls of a company where I had such a stellar reputation for nearly four years. What exactly was being said about me now that I was gone?

The most hurtful disconnection, however, was from

Anger—This is Not Who I Want to Be

Kristen. We were still connected on LinkedIn, but we usually didn't communicate with one another on that platform. Our regular correspondence was texting and calling each other multiple times throughout the day. In the days after my layoff, we texted just as much as we normally did. Messages ranged from the simplest of her sending good morning and well wishes for a great day to me sending her pictures of my newly put up Christmas decorations. I was trying to keep myself busy around the house doing normal things I would have been doing if I had not been laid off. Since Christmas was a few weeks away, I shared pictures of my decorated tree. Nothing was out of the ordinary from our communication. We kept the texts lighthearted. I began sharing with her ideas I had for what I wanted to do in my next chapter of my career by starting a sales advisory consultancy.

And then I got real with her in a text exchange:

> ME: If you prefer to never talk about work with me again I understand. Just tell me.

> KRISTEN: I don't see a world in which we will never talk about work again, I just don't know how I would react or what I would do if I was in your position, so it's hard for me to give advice as to what I think is right. I am still speechless.

> ME: Do you find it ironic that you were so worried and I was the one let go?

The Layoff Cooties – It's Them, Not You

> **KRISTEN:** Yeah of course I find it ironic.

> **ME:** I talked to some more folks today. They were very upset about how it all went down. A lot of people (outside of our team) are reaching out. I am getting the help I need so please don't feel I will be inundating you with this. I'm just very concerned you won't be my friend anymore.

> **KRISTEN:** Laura, our friendship is stronger than work. Never be concerned about that. I'm here for you as a friend AND you will never be forgotten. I don't feel like you're inundating me. I am still trying to process this … you tell me how I can support you as a friend.

> **ME:** I guess just check in on me. The roller coaster of emotions is very intense. One minute I think I'm fine. Next I'm enraged. I cannot sleep more than 2 hours at a time. I'm livid that I was the one who drew the short straw.

> **KRISTEN:** I will check in on you absolutely. I can imagine the changes of emotions hour by hour. And it's so fresh and unexpected. Processing it all … I'm doing the same so I can't even imagine what's going through your head.

Anger—This is Not Who I Want to Be

> ME: I'm not going to lie. There is a part of me that is jealous of you still being there. I just feel so disrespected. Gordon was so "I don't care about you" on my termination call. I'm just so concerned we're not going to be as close.

> KRISTEN: I don't want you to think like that AT ALL. Nor should you ever be jealous of anything. You have accomplished so much in your life and cannot think or compare against anyone else seriously. Nothing is going to change for our friendship. We are still going to be close and I care about you so much. Our bond is more than work!

> ME: Promise?

> KRISTEN: YES!

Seeing how others were disconnecting from me, I was worried about the narrative Kristen was hearing when someone mentioned my name. Gordon no longer wanted me on his leadership team, but Kristen still worked with Gordon, and I worried she would feel the need to distance herself from anything to do with me to preserve her job. I convinced myself to cut ties with her, thinking that would be best for us both.

In a moment of my devastation, I tested Kristen. I convinced myself it needed to be done. I was feeling horrible about

The Layoff Cooties – It's Them, Not You

myself, and I didn't want to bring her down with me. She had a bright sales future ahead of her, and clearly I wasn't supposed to be a part of it anymore. At least not at that company.

I had always tried to protect Kristen.

It was the Mama Bear mentality in our relationship.

So, on the evening of December 5th, 2023, just two days after Kristen promised we would always be friends, I sent her this text message:

> I think it is best if we part ways. I wish you well, Kristen.

I believed Kristen when she texted her loyalty to me and our friendship. I had no reason not to believe she would ever stop communicating with me. She had always shown up for me when I needed her before, so why wouldn't she continue to be the loyal friend she had shown herself to be for the previous two years?

Layoffs alter people. The ones laid off, and the ones left behind.

They make them do things one would never expect.

It's called self-preservation.

The next day, I regretted sending Kristen what I had texted her.

I was not thinking clearly.

Why did I send her this text?

It's not what I wanted.

I wanted her *in* my life, not *out* of it.

She had become one of my best friends.

Who was I to throw that away in my moment of grief and desperation?

Anger—This is Not Who I Want to Be

The emotions of everything that happened in the previous week were messing with my head. More importantly, why wasn't she responding with a *WTF was that text all about?* Why wasn't she fighting for our friendship?

I called her. I emailed her. I texted her:

> I was hoping to speak with you to explain my last text message. I don't want that to be the last thing between us, so if you can please find time this week to give me a call back, I would greatly appreciate it.

December 6th, no response.
December 7th, no response.
December 8th, no response.
We never went that long without corresponding.

The weekend of December 9th and 10th I sent pictures of food, my family, *anything* to get a response from Kristen. I sent more emails. I called, and it went straight to voicemail. I knew she was getting my texts. I sent DMs through LinkedIn.

The silence was deafening.

She was choosing to ignore me.

It was *her* choice. Not mine.

Yes, layoffs alter people. The ones laid off, and the ones left behind.

Yes, they make them do things one would never expect.

Yes, it's called self-preservation.

Was this Kristen's response to save herself in all this mess? I may never know, but it angered me because it didn't have to be this way.

7 Bargaining— What If versus Imagine If

In the months after my layoff, I couldn't help but replay many WHAT-IF scenarios in my mind about what I could have done differently.

Perhaps this was my fault.

Maybe I was too outspoken.

I guess I really wasn't the great leader everyone built me up to be.

The WHAT IF scenarios controlled my mind; I scribbled a bunch out one day to come up with a Top Ten List of WHAT IF, fill-in-the-blank-type questions. However, this Top Ten list was not as funny as the ones David Letterman used to share on late-night TV.

WHAT IF ... I never worked there in the first place?

WHAT IF ... I respected the chain of command?

WHAT IF ... I didn't ask so many questions?

WHAT IF ... I wasn't really a good leader?

WHAT IF... I just stayed in my lane?

Even if I came up with a list of one-hundred things I personally should have, could have, or would have done differently, it didn't change the fact that I lost my job. It was in the past. Dissecting this or that choice would not move me forward.

The Layoff Cooties – It's Them, Not You

What I can say is that I wouldn't have changed how I showed up to work every single day, working for the company that eventually would lay me off. I've always cared more about the Laura Krauss brand than any company brand I represented. If I upheld my personal brand with my set of core values, I'd be a model employee no matter where I worked.

I was proud, however, to represent my former company's core values because I believed in them too. And as shocking as it may sound, I still believed there were select individuals at my former company who were trying their damnedest to uphold those same values, despite the myriad of challenges.

Rehashing and reliving certain events in your mind can be a dangerous thing.

Conversations haunt you.

Images incite painful recollection of feelings from an exact moment in time.

You play the best hits of your worst hits over and over.

But it can also be tremendously healing; it's all about the reframe.

When I scribbled my Top Ten List of WHAT IF questions, I edited with a red pen weeks later, putting a line through the WHAT IF questions and thinking up IMAGINE IF ones instead.

Let me explain.

WHAT IF questions can carry a negative connotation. They inflict fear, doubt, and worry about the unknown.

IMAGINE IF questions offer a more positive connotation. They create a sense of wonder, possibility, and success.

Let's use a few examples to highlight the reframe:

- WHAT IF ... I never complained about my compensation versus IMAGINE IF my speaking up influenced changes in pay equity after my departure?
- WHAT IF ... I never agreed to mentor Kristen versus IMAGINE IF she can take our mentorship learnings and replicate that with other women?
- WHAT IF ... I never left a sales rep role moving into leadership versus IMAGINE IF my tenure as a leader influenced everyone on my team to believe in themselves for the first time in their careers?

See how simple a reframe of WHAT IF versus IMAGINE IF could be?

I learned this game-changing mindset on a professional development webinar with an executive coach a few years ago, and it stuck with me ever since. I used it when instilling belief with others on my sales team. Now I was using it to instill belief in myself.

Bargaining Dilemma #1:

Not Caring vs. Caring

The reality of being numbered in a statistic as someone laid off was not something I ever imagined defining my experience in corporate America.

WHAT IF I had never been laid off versus IMAGINE IF I can take this experience and be a beacon of hope and enlightenment for thousands of others who have been through a similar situation?

Would I even care about this growing population if it never happened to me?

The answer is no.

The Layoff Cooties – It's Them, Not You

I wouldn't have cared.

And I am not afraid to admit it either.

When the first few rounds of layoffs happened in the first half of 2023, I didn't think much of it. I knew layoffs would be part of our new PE firm's playbook because it is a standard operating procedure. I had experienced it at two other companies in my career, but I was never on the receiving end of a layoff from those tenures. I'm ashamed to say I always assumed the people who experienced layoffs would be upset for a few days, dust themselves off, update their resume, and go find their next job.

Easy-peasy. Not my problem. Let me get back to whatever I was doing.

Until it happens to you.

It's not that easy. It becomes your problem. You can't even remember what you were doing.

Rejection is still rejection.

It draws out visceral emotions you never knew existed until the rejection hits you directly. Feeling unwanted, especially when you enjoyed the work you were doing and were excellent at it, not only does it slam the pocketbook, but it strikes a traumatic blow to the ego and self-identity.

You question yourself on EVERYTHING.

Things that you are confident in, you no longer feel worthy. Skills in which you are strong, you second-guess whether they're really that sharp. Effort you knew you gave at 110 percent suddenly feels like maybe you were slacking. There's not a part of your identity that your mind doesn't analyze repeatedly when you experience rejection from your former employer.

Why do we do that to ourselves?
It's THEM, not US.

Bargaining Dilemma #2

Not Reaching Out vs. Reaching Out
I'm embarrassed to say I never reached out to colleagues who experienced a layoff. I don't even think it ever crossed my mind to contact them. As someone who considers herself an empathetic person, I'm ashamed to admit this endearing quality lapsed when it was needed most. After my layoff, I reached out to former colleagues laid off in earlier rounds and apologized for not contacting them sooner. I surprised a few folks by even calling, but everyone appreciated the sentiment.

Never feel like it's too late to reach out.

A simple text.

A quick voice mail.

A coffee chat over Zoom.

People will receive every gesture.

I promise you that.

WHAT IF you stayed quiet and said nothing versus IMAGINE IF you made someone's day better from your outreach?

WHAT IF you apologized, and they didn't accept it versus IMAGINE IF they felt cared about and you did too?

See how powerful WHAT IF versus IMAGINE IF can be toward healing your soul?

The Layoff Cooties – It's Them, Not You

Bargaining Dilemma #3

Being Forgotten vs. Not Being Forgotten

My deepest fear was being forgotten at the company whose colors I had bled for nearly four years. I cared so much about my professional legacy.

WHAT IF I'm forgotten in the day-to-day grind versus IMAGINE IF people never forget the impact I had on even just one interaction with them?

I am choosing the latter.

I know I mattered. Not only to the bottom line, but to the hundreds of people I interacted with over the course of nearly four years.

I was a top-performing sales professional. Customers loved working with me, and internal stakeholders enjoyed partnering with me to win deals and overcome challenges.

I was the sales leader people wanted to follow. Reps from other teams booked time on my calendar to get advice on strategy for their deals or to talk through an issue because they weren't getting the support they needed from their manager. I filled the leadership void.

I helped people believe. Believe in themselves, believe in our company, believe in doing the right thing.

I motivated others. To be better, to strive for more, and to never give up.

I brought fun and laughter to a very challenging working environment.

I "listened with my eyes" with customers to walk them down from a cliff when conflicts arose. Just how many customer renewals would I help save the company? More than anyone would ever know. Behind the scenes. Up the corporate ladder.

I solved problems. Not just mine, but others. By bringing together alternative viewpoints to gain consensus on the best course of action. Because differing views foster communication, which is far better than not knowing anyone's viewpoints at all.

I spoke up when no one else would. Because it was the right thing to do, and it needed to be said. Let the consequences be what they must. I lay my head on my pillow at night, knowing I did what was morally and ethically right. And that's a kind of peace I will seek wherever I work.

WHAT IF I AM FORGOTTEN?
IMAGINE IF I AM NOT.
What if you're not forgotten?
Imagine, you're not.

8 Depression— Been There, Done That

I was determined to not allow my layoff to spiral me into a depression. I tried to keep busy as much as I could in the first few days after that life altering moment. Going from a full calendar of back-to-back meetings and never-ending to-do lists to a completely open calendar numbs you. Suddenly you realize those to-do lists really mean nothing at all. Someone else is now responsible for those meetings on your calendar.

To-do list. Complete.

Not my problem anymore.

Since time was on my side, I defaulted into "Mom" mode 100 percent of my time. Laundry? I would do it. Grocery shopping? I could go in the middle of the day! Kelsie needed a ride to school? No worries. I would take her. And pick her up. My time was suddenly everyone else's time because let's face it. I didn't have a "real job" anymore to take me away from home responsibilities.

Less than a week after my layoff, I dropped Kelsie off at Youth Night at our church. Every Tuesday evening, from 6:30 to 8:30 p.m., middle school kids gather for a fun night of events as part of their youth group church program. Erik was at Ben's high school basketball game in a neighboring town so they wouldn't be home until close to 10:00 p.m.

The Layoff Cooties – It's Them, Not You

Everything went as planned. I dropped Kelsie off and told her I'd be back later.

In between those two hours, however, I was not in a good place mentally. I spent the entire time lying in bed, reading old text messages from colleagues and reliving the play-by-play of receiving the 9:15 a.m. email, joining the faceless Zoom call with Gordon, and having my system access removed shortly thereafter. I couldn't stop crying about how unfair it all seemed. I sent a few heart-wrenching texts to friends, letting them know I was struggling. Remember when I said layoffs change people? It was during this time block I sent the text to Kristen saying, "I think it is best if we part ways." I was spiraling downward and acting erratically.

Before I knew it, 8:15 p.m. rolled around, and I had to pick up Kelsie. I needed to pull myself together. My eyes were bloodshot from crying, and my hair was a complete mess. I grabbed a hat, put on my glasses, which I needed to drive anyway, and somehow drove myself safely down the road to get my daughter. Once I arrived, I realized I needed to go in and get her because the church youth group leaders don't allow the kids to walk out without their parents.

Greeeeeeeeeeaaat.

I looked like shit and had to find her in a sea of a hundred people.

Times like this are when you look your worst. You run into everyone (and their mother) when you're trying to slip in and out of somewhere incognito. My Wednesday night Bible study leader and dear friend Diane locked eyes with me and could see I was clearly upset. She started to walk my way. I quickly dismissed her by putting my hand up between us. I would later apologize for my rudeness, but at that moment I wasn't looking to explain my tears. Diane already knew why I was upset; she was the first person I called for support the day of my layoff just a few days prior.

I bolted straight toward the back of the room where my daughter was congregating with a group of kids. Kelsie could see I was in no position to hang around. As we walked out of the building and through the parking lot, she put her hand on my back and whispered, "Come on Mom, let's get you home." How is this eleven-year-old, pre-teen, middle-school child of mine acting like the mom in this situation? Just like Ben a few days earlier, when I shared my layoff news with him, Kelsie was taking her turn jumping into parent mode. I didn't know if it was innate or something she learned, but I certainly welcomed it. I can't tell you how I drove home that night. But I do remember telling Kelsie that I felt like a complete failure while we were in the car. A failure at everything in life.

Being a mom. Failure.

Being a wife. Failure.

Being a friend. Failure.

Being a regional vice president of sales. Absolute Failure.

I couldn't get these overwhelming feelings of failure out of my head.

When we got home, I unlocked the door to our house, and she followed me upstairs to my bedroom. She helped me get in bed—no need to change my clothes—and tucked me in for the night as I sobbed into my pillow. She kissed me on my forehead, shut off the light, closed my bedroom door and retreated to her room next to mine, waiting for Erik and Ben to get home.

The Layoff Cooties – It's Them, Not You

I wanted to stay in bed in a fetal position for as long as I could. And for that night, that's exactly what I did. Some would say that's a poor way to handle things and others would say that's just what the doctor ordered. The key would be ensuring I didn't have too many of those lying-in-a-fetal-position moments because I had a life to live. I just needed to find a new normal. I would not let any form of depression sink in because there was too much at stake.

I knew what depression looked and felt like.

Been there. Done that.

Not interested in doing it again.

I already had experienced far too many depressive times before my mid-forties.

When I was a junior in college, I struggled with depression about my future. I wondered if my chosen course of study was going to yield the successful business career I wanted as a little girl. I attended a small, private liberal arts school in the Roanoke Valley, and with less than two-thousand students, you couldn't go to the bathroom without someone knowing. The small-town college community felt like a bubble. Despite having many friends, starring on the women's soccer team, and serving as a leader and treasurer for my Chi Omega sorority, my senior year of college couldn't come fast enough.

I nearly didn't go to my junior year spring sorority dance because I didn't have a date. However, my roommate's boyfriend invited his friend, who went to neighboring Virginia Tech, to go to the dance with me. I wound up having a great time because I had no expectations. That evening, I won the coveted "Sister of the Year" award as a junior, a huge surprise for me because a senior sorority sister usually received the honor.

Even in my worst moments, when I couldn't see my greatness, others could, and they reminded me often of the positive ripple effect I had on those around me.

I found myself in another depression in 2003. Erik was living out West, studying for his master degree in accounting at Colorado State University. (Go, RAMS!) We were technically "on a break," but were still friends with benefits, if you know what I mean. He wanted me to date other people, which pissed me off because I didn't want to be with anyone else. *Who the hell was he to decide that I should date other people?* He wound up coming to his senses after graduation. I guess he earned a master degree in accounting and common sense.

When I found out I was pregnant with Ben, less than a month after Erik and I were married in 2005, I faced bouts of depression yet again. Erik and I had gotten engaged, married, built a house, started new jobs, moved into our new house, and found out we were expecting our first kid in less than a year's time. My immediate pregnancy less than a month after we were married was not part of "our master plan," but looking back now, and knowing how Ben blessed our lives and Kelsie six years later, I wouldn't have changed a thing.

But the greatest episode of depression came during one of the worst economic times our country had seen. Erik and I left highly successful careers in 2007 and 2008 in pursuit of the American dream: to own a business. We invested heavily, both financially and emotionally, in what we believed was an important step in securing our family's future. No one could have predicted the perfect economic storm when we opened a DirectBuy franchise in Hagerstown, Maryland, in January 2009. The challenges we would face running a multi-million-dollar business were unknown to us. While we had many successes in the two years we were open, the realization that the business model couldn't sustain itself over time overshadowed our aspirations. In hindsight, our small market territory never should have been a viable franchise for anyone to open, let alone the two of us.

Less than three months after we opened, it was clear we had made a tremendous mistake. I suddenly felt solely responsible for our situation, as I was the one who spearheaded the business plan to invest in the franchise. The result was a business model that provided zero work-life balance. Erik's parents raised Ben because we were at work all the time, and I had little satisfaction in any area of my life, professionally or personally.

By September 2009, less than nine months after opening, I found myself in a deep clinical depression. I felt like a complete failure in every aspect of my life: I had borrowed a significant amount of money from family, which I felt I could not repay in their lifetime; I saw Ben less than twenty-four waking hours a week; my body was deteriorating to a low of ninety-five pounds because of a lack of interest in eating and sleep deprivation; my marriage was platonic, if that, and my positive, I-can-do-anything attitude reflected a distant memory of someone I didn't even recognize in the mirror. This was not the life I imagined, and I didn't feel I could go on any further.

By October 2009, I was meeting with a therapist once a week to talk through my issues. I never had a problem discussing how I felt about my life's decisions, and denial never was a stage that I traveled on my road to recovery.

I held myself accountable for the situation I was in and sincerely felt there was no way out. My therapist decided the best solution was to start a series of antidepressant and sleeping pill prescriptions. I opposed this form of treatment because I feared the prescriptive combination would lead to a dangerous outcome. But I followed my physician's advice. The doctor gave me concurrent prescriptions of Prozac, Seroquel, and Ambien. Prozac (a popular antidepressant) and Ambien (a prescriptive sleeping aid) probably don't require explanation, but I feel the Seroquel prescription does. It's an antipsychotic drug prescribed for bipolar disorder, which was not my diagnosis, and I didn't display any symptoms, but my physician prescribed it to ease my anxiety and sleep deprivation. The doctor should never have given me that prescription. The small dosage per pill knocked out my frail body for over twelve hours. And yet, I followed the doctor's advice and took my "happy pills."

I am not disparaging prescription medication, as I know millions of people benefit from antidepressant drugs, but it was not the answer for me. During the next two months, I went in and out of three hospitals as part of my depression treatment. I was mentally and physically exhausted. I couldn't bear the thought of salvaging our franchise any longer. I popped pills because they afforded me the silence and luxury of sleep. I had no responsibility when I was asleep, and I could hurt no one, including myself.

On Christmas Eve in 2009, I reached my lowest desperation point. We traveled to my parent's house on Long Island to spend a few days for the holidays. Knowing that I would attend a Christmas Eve celebration at my sister's house later that evening, I swallowed a handful of pills earlier in the day, hoping I wouldn't awaken. Thankfully, I woke up. My family did not know what I attempted. The mix of prescription medications, however, caused me to hallucinate, and I fell flat on my face in my parent's kitchen. I suffered trauma to my teeth and mouth area, along with a cut above my right eye. I probably should have sought medical attention, but it was Christmas Eve, and I'm sure the hospital was the last place my family wanted to spend the holiday. The resulting scar above my eye serves as a daily reminder of a time and place that I never want to go back to—and it was from that point forward I knew my life would change forever.

God had given me a second chance. It wasn't my time. There was more work to be done.

My family remembers that time as the worst holiday season on record, but I view them as successful steps toward restoring my health. I stopped taking the depression and bipolar medication and began regular acupuncture sessions and massage therapy. Slowly, I began gaining weight and sleeping again at night, without medication. I achieved this with the belief that I wasn't getting better for myself; I was doing it for others. My husband, my son, my parents, my siblings, my friends—anyone *but* myself. By focusing on others, it helped to ease the stress I was going through.

I began reading positive books to fill my mind with optimism instead of pessimism. And I slowly realized that while opening our business didn't happen overnight, closing it down wouldn't happen as quickly either. In 2010, we kept our franchise open for business each month by generating enough revenue to employ eight to ten part-time and full-time staff, to pay our bills timely and efficiently, and to compensate ourselves enough to protect our home life.

Depression—Been There, Done That

There were good days and bad days, but I knew deep down, after all that I had endured, life would only get better with time.

By Christmas Eve in 2010, we enjoyed the holiday season much more after experiencing the horror of the previous year. Erik and I agreed to make preparations to close our business in the most practical way possible. At the start of 2011, we met with a bankruptcy attorney and learned how easy it would be to file for protection under these laws. Once we knew what we were facing, closing our franchise wasn't a difficult decision. We struggled to open and operate a business in one of this world's toughest economies. Declaring bankruptcy was very simple. We would start anew with a clean slate and rebuild our lives. We closed our doors on January 8, 2011, five days short of our two-year anniversary of opening DirectBuy of Hagerstown, Maryland.

Erik and I collected unemployment benefits for nearly three months before we both found jobs again in our pre-franchise disciplines. Unemployment benefits served their intended purpose, and we were grateful. By the end of May 2011, we were in new industries and capitalizing on the skill sets we had learned from opening and operating a business. We recovered the financial means we had before franchise ownership and slowly began paying back our family loans while sustaining the needs of our growing family.

I knew what rock bottom felt like.

I knew what starting over meant.

I knew what was required to combat my depression.

Looking back to that time in my life, I knew there was no way a layoff was going to spiral me down in that direction again.

Regardless of how hurt I was to have lost my dream job, my multi-six figure W-2, and my work friendships in what I believed was a targeted and politically motivated layoff, depression was not an option.

This time, I had my faith in God.

This time, I knew the value of my family.

This time, I would use my experience to help others rejected by a layoff.

There's power in that. I just needed to tap into it.

The more I talked about what happened with my layoff with other people, the better I felt. Getting the words out and sharing my pain with others fulfilled my healing needs. The more vulnerable posts I would write on LinkedIn, the greater healing power I would feel releasing it into the world.

Almost immediately, I got multiple requests from complete strangers to jump on a Zoom for thirty minutes to share layoff stories with one another. After one post with the hook line, "The Gut Punches of a Layoff," I had over forty meetings booked in the subsequent weeks with people wanting to chat. Many times, the thirty-minute calls would turn into hour-long conversations or follow-up Zooms the next week to continue the chat. These are metrics that counting LinkedIn impressions and engagements and on a line graph can't measure. These metrics filled my soul in a priceless way that no chart could ever capture. To this day, I have kept in touch with many of the people I've met through my LinkedIn posts after sharing my vulnerable layoff story. I consider them dear friends who I would have never met had my former company not laid me off on November 29, 2023, at 9:15 a.m.

There's nothing depressing about that at all.

9 Testing—Does Anyone Really Know What Works?

Everyone has their way of testing how they manage grief. They create coping mechanisms to function and work through the difficult times. For some, it's as simple as getting through the day. They may choose to engage in self-destructive behavior like drinking or drugs. I'm not advocating for that, but it's easy to see how people can reach a point when hope seems lost. I love a glass of wine now and then, but when I drank a bottle of wine by myself a few nights after my layoff, the only thing it did for me was give me a hangover the next day. That's not how I want to spend my future, thank you very much.

My coping mechanism became productivity. You know, getting things done. Feeling like I accomplished something and having something to show for it. In the months after my layoff, I kept myself busy by not thinking about anything work related. I didn't have those work commitments anymore, so why waste time thinking about them? Time was now on my side to spend my days as I wanted without having to log into a computer for back-to-back virtual meetings or traveling up and down the East Coast of the United States and in Canada visiting customers. The shift from a full calendar of responsibilities that defined my purpose became a blank slate of time.

For me, the first step in coping came with the realization that I'm never going to get *over* this traumatic experience. The only way to heal is *through*. One day at a time. My timeline won't be the same as yours. It's not supposed to be. Please don't compare.

There are defining moments that serve as mile markers and turning points in our lives. And there are things we do to test ourselves to cope with pushing forward toward acceptance.

The layoff is a mile marker in my life. Pre-layoff versus post layoff. At one point, bankruptcy was a mile marker too. Pre-franchise ownership versus post-franchise ownership. We all have mile markers in our lives. If we are truly honest, we can acknowledge them without fear. It is what it is. They happened when they happened. The important thing is what we DO with what happened to us.

In this chapter, I'm sharing some things I did to keep myself busy in the weeks and months after my layoff. I never forgot the situation, but I used my newfound open calendar as an opportunity to do things I historically felt too busy to do when I held a full-time job. As you read through the ways I stayed productive, I challenge you to think about the possibilities of doing the same. What ways could you test to cope with this newfound change in employment status?

Decluttering my house helped declutter my mind:
One of the first things I did was clean my house. Not just dusting and vacuuming, but getting rid of stuff. I used my layoff as an opportunity to minimize material things accumulated over twenty years. I went from room to room, emptying closets, rearranging drawers, and throwing out

things we had not used in years. If it didn't serve a purpose right then and there, or soon, I tossed it.

Before my layoff, we were planning to renovate our unfinished basement. Our contractor was lined up to start after the new year. After the layoff, we scrapped those plans and saved the money we planned to dump into the renovation. Even though we earmarked money for this project, it didn't seem prudent to move forward. We had lived in our home for twenty years without a finished basement; we could continue for the unforeseeable future without one. I still, however, wanted to purge many things in our basement. I spent a few days after the Christmas and New Year holidays alone in the basement sorting through boxes of pictures, forgotten college mementos, old toys and accumulated household junk that piled up over the years. I was so proud of my cleaned-out basement I texted a photo to our contractor letting him know it was ready for him ... in a few more years.

The next big cleanse was our master bedroom closet. When Erik and I built our home in 2005, we made sure we had a large walk-in closet, not only for our wardrobes but for ample shelving and storage space. Neither of us are clothes whores, but we hold on to items until they either have holes in them or until old style trends have returned. We are in our mid-to-late forties and still have clothing items from college! Yikes.

I started on my side of the closet. I had the dress I wore the day I closed my largest deal as a sales rep back at SAP Concur in 2017. That deal catapulted me toward earning Mid-Market Rep of the Year. It hung in my closet, although I couldn't fit into it anymore. Whenever I looked at that dress, I remembered how good it felt as I memorialized a career milestone I was proud to achieve.

Is that silly? Maybe.

Next to the dress was the soft pink cardigan sweater I was wearing the day of the layoff. The infamous picture I took when I was on camera for my termination call, and Gordon was too much of a coward to turn on his video, captured that sweater. It hung in my closet, and even though it still fit, I'd probably never wear it again. Whenever I looked at it, I remembered how disrespected I felt. A pink cardigan memorialized a career marker I never thought I'd experience.

Is that silly? Maybe.

Clearly, I still had an emotional attachment to both the dress and sweater. I put them both in the donation pile on my bedroom floor. Kelsie joined me in this purging exercise. She loves organizing and cleaning; mix in going through clothing too? It made for a fun mother-daughter bonding experience. I'd try things on; she'd give me a thumbs up or thumbs down. Actually, it was more like a smile or a sneer. Yes, I was taking fashion advice from my eleven-year-old. Don't judge. She has way more style than I do!

When we finished sorting, I had three garbage-sized bags to donate to my church's upcoming clothing drive. *One person's trash is another person's treasure*, as they say. I mumbled a prayer over the clothing items that reminded me of my work milestones and asked God to ensure someone else could use them to feel empowered and confident when wearing them. I asked Him to take away that negative energy around the sweater and bless it with new life. These items served a purpose for me in my career; now it was time for them to serve someone else in a positive way. This seemed like a perfect example to remember that we don't know the ripple effect our actions can have on someone else. Perhaps that sweater is what someone else needs to feel comforted, warm, and secure. Or better yet, perhaps a person will wear that sweater to a job interview and get the job because they felt confident in it. Yes, that's a much better memory for me to keep. Thanks, God.

Volunteering is good for the soul:
Once I cleaned out every nook and cranny of my home, I explored ways to volunteer. When I had my bouts of depression over the years, I often searched for opportunities to serve others to train my focus on someone else. I had always wanted to lead a Bible-based growth group at my church, but I never felt confident in any scriptural knowledge to feel worthy enough to lead a class.

With time on my hands, I realized that God's not looking for perfection; He's looking for participants, and I was willing and able to show up and say YES!

Enter Financial Peace University (FPU).

FPU is a financial literacy course created by Dave Ramsey. Many churches promote the program because of the biblical references on how we should think and handle the money God has entrusted us with. Before you jump out of your seats, I've read books by Suze Orman, Tori Dunlap, and other financial gurus. I had never been a Dave Ramsey disciple, but I liked how he connected faith and finances.

I never completed FPU's famous "The 7 Baby Steps" money management program, and I'm not advocating you go out and buy his program or listen to his podcast. I always had an interest in personal finance and helped several friends get out of debt over the years. On top of that, I thought teaching FPU through my local church would be a great way to volunteer, lead a faith-based growth group, and give me something to look forward to each week.

I met with the program director of our church's growth groups and asked if I could teach FPU for the winter session scheduled from the end of January through early April 2024. Except I had a twist. I wanted to offer the class only to women. Usually, people take the course in a co-ed environment. I felt strongly there was an unmet need, whereby some women were hesitant to speak about their finances in a mixed setting. I thought they may open up in a group of like-minded women.

I was right.

Once enrollment opened for the winter session, the class filled quickly with a group of women twenty-two to sixty-eight years of age. Married. Divorced. Single. Children. No children. Blue collar. White collar. No retirement money saved. Some retirement money saved. What's retirement money?

These women had a major impact on me over ten weeks.

They took the first step to improve their financial education and change their negative behaviors toward money by asking for help. I'm not a financial advisor, but I was confident in teaching a lesson plan and communicating a system that works. I knew how to motivate others. To inspire. To build belief. I couldn't be prouder of them, and I count all of them as friends today.

This is my PSA to volunteer. You have talents to share with this world. And the confidence you can gain from helping other people is real. You will feel better, and they will be grateful. A win-win situation. Volunteering provided another way for me to continue leading others.

Leadership is simply influence. You don't need a paid title to give yourself fully, freely, and forever. Remember: God's not looking for perfection; He's looking for participants. Are you willing and able to show up and say yes?

What if you ignored the call to volunteer your time and talents? *Imagine* the lives that would be changed, *if* you didn't.

My favorite coping mechanism–personal and professional development:

When my former company promoted me to a regional vice president role in 2022, I invested more in my personal and professional development. I never worked for a company that put their corporate dollars into me as an individual contributor or as a leader. I had plenty of self-help books on my shelf and they inspired me for a short period of time, but I wanted something that went beyond the pages of a book. I wanted connections with people.

My Chief network provided plenty of opportunities to meet many high-powered, ambitious, and motivational female coaches and leaders. I attended a few Chief events when traveling for business in the New York City area and brought Kristen along for the ride. I wanted her to see the benefits of the Chief network and meet other women who could inspire her potentially. Pay it forward, right?

In January 2023, Kristen and I attended a book signing event where we met Jennie Blumenthal, a fellow Chief member and also a good friend of my friend Kara (the one who introduced me to Erik). Kara had sent Jennie an email right before the holidays introducing us. Jennie and I never

The Layoff Cooties – It's Them, Not You

connected, even though we lived less than an hour from each other. Now I had an opportunity to hear Jennie speak at an event where she was promoting her book, *Corporate Rehab: Ditch the Hustle Culture and Thrive Again*. I wanted to reintroduce myself, this time in person, and of course support her work. Kristen and I waited in line to meet Jennie and the other women promoting their books. Jennie was so gracious in those few moments that I decided right then to work with her.

Later that spring, I signed up for Jennie's coaching program called THRIVE. Over the next few months, I committed to completing the pre-work exercises before each session and shared my growing pains and challenges with her as I continued my corporate leadership journey. I voiced all my professional concerns during our time together: the misgivings from all the PE changes as our company went from public to private; the lack of authority I was being given in hiring the people I wanted to build out my team; the pay inequity issues that were rampant in our sales organization; the sadness I felt losing Kristen on my team to her own leadership role before finishing what we had started; and the political drama that never seemed to end.

You name it; we discussed it.

Her thought-provoking sessions clarified how I could be a better leader. I was happy to invest both the time and money into the program. I don't know what I would have done without her guidance in those final months of my leadership role. (Well, I didn't know at the time they were my final months.)

Our final session was supposed to be in early November 2023. With a last-minute scheduling conflict, I rescheduled for a few weeks later. By the time we regrouped in early December, the company had laid me off. Jennie helped me plan for my next act, which was to start my sales advisory consultancy. She recommended people and resources she used to get her coaching business up and running and made introductions where it made sense. Although our time together in a formal executive coaching program expired, she cheered me on and believed in me as I transitioned into my next chapter.

As I started posting daily on LinkedIn after my layoff, my connections and network grew. At first I connected more with other Chiefs and set up one-on-one meetings with many of them. Suzanne Roske was another Chief member based in the Washington, D.C. area like me and was also a former colleague of Jennie's during their time as partners at PWC. Suzanne had written a book called, *I'm Supposed to Be Doing This: An Adult Gap Year*. It was her story about deciding to leave her executive partner role and move her family to Oaxaca, Mexico for a year during the pandemic. It's an easy read I finished in one afternoon and evening. I emailed Suzanne, letting her know how much her book resonated with me. Even though she left her career and a former company snatched mine away, there were many parallels that pulled at my heartstrings such as feelings of self-worth tied to a career, losing identity once the job ends, and the longing to find the best version of ourselves—for families and ourselves.

Suzanne transitioned from being a partner at PWC to starting her own executive coaching company called Vamonos Executive Coaching. She was planning a transformational retreat in Oaxaca, Mexico, in March 2024.

This time, she was bringing a group of eight women with her. I had never been to Mexico outside of Cancun when I traveled there for a President's Club trip for my former company. This Oaxaca trip was in a region of Mexico I probably never would have visited on my own. The thought of immersing myself in a transformational retreat with other women also trying to figure out who they are? Sure. Why not?

I had accumulated enough frequent flier miles to have my flights already paid for, and I used part of my severance money to invest in this trip. I was a little nervous to go by myself, so I asked my sister if she wanted to join in the fun. Erica has traveled to nearly sixty countries during her lifetime and walked on all seven continents. This avid adventurer and explorer was always up for a trip somewhere around the world. Surprisingly, she had never been to this region of Mexico either, so it was relatively easy to get her buy in.

YOLO! (You Only Live Once ... explaining the acronym for my octogenarian mother)!

Erica was hesitant about the coaching sessions before, during, and after the trip because she had never worked with an executive coach in this capacity. My sister was at a crossroads in her career as well, and I think this gave her an opportunity to talk through what her next phase of professional life would be like after her retirement from higher education.

Before I knew it, we both signed up for the inaugural Vamonos Experience, traveling to Oaxaca, Mexico for a week in mid-March 2024.

Prior to leaving for Mexico, I had two coaching sessions with Suzanne so we could identify areas of opportunity for growth during our time at the retreat. I couldn't wait for these formal sessions to begin. I'm an open book and will talk about anything and everything at any time someone is ready to chat. There's no question I'm unwilling to answer. I had already completed a questionnaire filled with things Suzanne wanted to know about me both personally and professionally prior to this call.

Within minutes of our Zoom call, however, I was in tears. Suzanne asked me a question, and I either was at a loss for words, or my response was "I don't know" as I fought back the tears.

This was so unlike me.

I thought I had been doing a good job handling my emotions as of late.

It had been three months since my layoff.

I broke down crying with Suzanne.

I felt like a complete idiot.

This is not how I wanted our first session to go!

I couldn't help but think: *this woman will not be excited to spend a week with me south of the border after this conversation*!

We talked a lot about my relationship with Kristen since that's where so much of my grief was stemming. Our mentorship journey toward friendship. The hurt I felt with Kristen's silence and lack of response to my outreach so soon after my layoff. It all hurt so damn much.

Suzanne suggested Kristen most likely put our relationship in a box and perhaps that was her way of compartmentalizing our relationship and not dealing with her own trauma. You know, her own self-preservation. We talked through if maybe it would serve me well to put the relationship in a container too. I could always go back and open it up to revisit it, but it didn't need to sit with me every day. Initially,

The Layoff Cooties – It's Them, Not You

this seemed like not dealing with the emotions of it all, but it definitely was a different perspective from anything I had thought about before where Kristen was concerned.

We ended the call, and I immediately texted Jennie:

> ME: I just had a therapy session with Suzanne. It was a great coaching session but she caught me on an emotional day.

> JENNIE: I'm really glad to hear it! I know this layoff happened at the end of our coaching time together but this stuff takes a while to process and there may be more emotional days ahead. My pep talk for the morning: don't run from it. The emotions are just signals-from you, to you-and they are here to tell you something.

Signals.
FROM you. TO you.
I loved that explanation.

I felt the signals. I felt the signals in a million different directions *from* me and *to* me.

God always has a way of bringing people in and out of my life, and these two women exemplified that. Even though I was in tears, I felt blessed and grateful knowing I had these two supportive Chiefs on my side.

The Vamonos Experience to Oaxaca, Mexico, couldn't have come at a better time of year. March is usually when I was on a President's Club trip with my former employer.

Testing—Does Anyone Really Know What Works?

President's Club trips are incentives earned by sales professionals for outperforming their annual quotas. It's an all-expense-paid vacation with a guest of your choice for a few days, usually to some exotic, all-inclusive resort. I had taken these trips multiple times with my former employer and throughout my sales career as a top performer. I knew I'd start seeing posts on LinkedIn, so going on my trip around the same time made perfect sense to me. Ironically, my former employer's recipients were celebrating in Mexico again this year too.

I will not lie. I thought about detouring to Cancun to show up at their poolside resort and say, "Oh my, I didn't know you guys would be here. It's so *great* to see you all again!" (Please read that with every inflection of sarcasm and passive aggressiveness you can muster).

I filled my Mexican retreat with margaritas and poolside activity at the Casa Lyobaa, a boutique hotel in Mitla, Oaxaca. But this time, it was part of a transformational trip to accelerate my next chapter. More than an all-inclusive vacation, the Vamonos Experience focused on four main areas: personal and leadership development, adventure and experience, community and connection, and holistic wellness.

Seven days and six nights of a healthy mix of all the above was what I needed. From a cacao welcoming ceremony, over twenty-five hours of individual and group coaching, experiencing an Oaxacan market food tour, hiking in La Sierra Norte de Oaxaca, San Antonio Cuajimoloyas, and the waterfalls of Hierve el Agua and Las Salinas, the retreat helped me appreciate the many blessings in my life. I was still grieving the layoff, of course, but I now had a renewed sense of seeing my life through a different lens. Immersing myself in an ancient culture helped me gain a new world perspective. *My new world.*

I recognize this trip came with extreme privilege. Many of you reading this are probably thinking, "OK, it must be nice to be laid off and take a trip to Mexico a few months later." I get it; my path isn't exactly everyone's realistic remedy toward reassessing their next chapter in life. I was fortunate to be in this position, so you better believe I was going to make the most of my time there.

With that said, you don't need to hop on a plane to find yourself in another country to cope. There are activities you can do stateside in the comfort of your home to reevaluate your next steps after a layoff. (I share some of these exercises and activities in Chapter 11: From Rejection to Redirection).

With all the fun activities on the agenda in Mexico, hiking was the one thing I was *least* looking forward to. There were two of them, and I needed to prepare myself mentally to complete both that week. Let's just say if you were to ask my best friends from college how much I loved hiking, they can tell you horrific stories from our youthful days hiking in the Roanoke Valley. I was not what you would call a happy hiker. My collegiate hikes were over twenty-five years ago, so surely I had matured in my mental acuity and hiking ability since that time? Maybe. Maybe not.

I trusted Suzanne had done her due diligence to vet these mountainside hikes for our diverse group of women. She described them as moderately difficult trails. OK, I could handle that. There would be plenty of opportunities to stop along the way, lots of water breaks, and beautiful photo opportunities at every glance despite the colder, rainier day we were expecting. Midway through the first hike, I was exhibiting those old collegiate, unhappy hiking thoughts. I guess I hadn't grown up after all. We weren't even halfway done, and the terrain grew steeper and wetter in more sections than I had anticipated.

I was tired.

Emotionally and physically.

We had two local hiking guides from the Sierra Norte who knew these trails. They were a father-daughter duo who grew up on this mountainside, proudly storytelling throughout the hike. (Thank goodness we had an interpreter because I don't know any Spanish outside of *hola* for hello and *adios* for goodbye).

We followed them in our small pack of women and, at times, formed a single line through the trails. At one point, our group split up; several women took a less strenuous trail with the daughter guide. I continued following the more difficult trail with the father. I don't know what irritated me, but there was one section where my sister tried to help me from behind to get through a hard part of the terrain. The rocks had formed a skinny entrance to climb through, but with the wet conditions, I wasn't confident in my footing and how to keep my balance. There were strategic spots to grab the rocks on either side, but I wasn't confident of finding them either.

My sister is an avid rock climber. This hike was nothing for her. She could probably do it in her sleep. I wanted none of her assistance as she tried to help me up a ravine.

"Get the fuck off me!" I turned and shouted in her face.

It was quiet, and I was not, so everyone heard me.

Yikes. Erica was only trying to help.

Why do we not accept help from those who love us?

The Layoff Cooties – It's Them, Not You

Do you struggle with that too?

I've often thought about why that is the case, and the only thing I can think of is that I want to appear strong, like I have everything under control. I want the people who know and love me to not worry about helping or taking care of me. But really, it's just the opposite. The people who love us the most are the ones who want to help. They want to take care of us if we will only let them. My sister was showing me she cared by helping me through a rough part of the hike, and I yelled obscenities in her face.

At that moment, I didn't pay attention to how my sister responded. It wasn't until later that I learned of the hurt I caused her in that split moment where I let my emotions get the best of me. She was probably embarrassed as others in our group turned to see what was going on between us. *Ooooh, the sisters were fighting.* Everyone loves juicy family drama, right?

Holly, a woman in front of me, offered her hand to help. I accepted her help graciously and listened to where she told me to put my hands and feet.

After several miles, there was a clearing during the hike where we had a beautiful view of the valley below. We rested on the rocks and began an exercise of writing a letter to ourselves. The hike was challenging because it forced me to be alone with my thoughts, even though people from our group surrounded us. Suzanne wanted us to be silent for parts of the hike and think about many of the prompts from our group coaching sessions earlier in the week.

I tried to think about many things besides my layoff, but it kept coming back to that. Most of all, my thoughts kept returning to my lost friendship with Kristen. Something as simple as this hike made me think about her. She enjoyed hiking when she would visit her dad in Arizona. If we were still friends, I knew she would enjoy making fun of me hiking if I sent her funny pics from the Mexican mountainside because she knew I didn't enjoy it. But I didn't have to worry about that. She would never see the pictures of my Mexican adventure. And I was pretty sure she was not thinking about me either.

Instead of writing a letter to myself, I wrote a letter to Kristen.

A goodbye letter, if you will.

I didn't know when I would send it to her, but writing her a letter saying exactly how I felt about how much her silence hurt me made me feel better. I probably could have saved a couple thousand bucks and written that letter stateside. But the clarity I found in myself on top of this mountain in Sierra Norte apparently was what I needed to take those feelings from my heart and place them into my Vamonos Experience workbook. The final version of that letter to Kristen is in the next chapter on acceptance. Perhaps she'll read it there too.

It wasn't until the next day, when we were in a group coaching session, that my sister revealed how hurt she felt when I wouldn't accept her help during the hike. She especially didn't appreciate my choice of words that everyone else heard too.

Ouch. I felt really bad. She didn't deserve my wrath at that moment. Or ever.

I apologized to her in that group setting. To her face. But in front of everyone.

She accepted my apology as a good big sister does.

The Layoff Cooties – It's Them, Not You

My outburst toward my sister was a coping mechanism. Right or wrong, it's how I dealt with the situation.

We all have coping mechanisms and things we try to test. Some are positive things, like staying productive by cleaning out a basement or closet, volunteering, or investing in personal or professional development. Some are negative things, like drinking a bottle of wine by yourself and swearing at your sister on the Mexican mountainside.

My point is this: they are *your* coping mechanisms and are unique to your grieving process as you test multiple things.

Don't compare your timeline, how you cope, and your layers of grief with anyone else's.

No one really knows what works.

That's why we're all testing different things.

It's up to you to figure out what works best for *you*.

10 Acceptance— The Gift I Gave Myself

Acceptance is not a final destination. There is no ending. It may be the final stage in the seven stages of grief as we've journeyed through this book, but I don't feel any finality in my grieving process upon arriving at this stage.

I've said it before, and I'll say it again: Grief is not something you get *over*. It's something you get *through*. Acceptance is the realization that:

1. Yes! This happened to me.
2. You know what? I'm going to be OK.

Part of my healing toward acceptance of what happened and the lost relationships I missed hinged on my ability to express myself through writing. Each written expression, whether from journaling, posting on LinkedIn, or writing this book, filled a void that healed my soul.

Besides the WHAT IF/IMAGINE IF exercises, I wrote letters to the people who were such a driving force in my tenure at my former company. I may never know if they will read this book. I most likely may never hear from any of them again, but these letters provided a sense of closure through expressing my final thoughts on what I would say to them if they were sitting in front of me today.

The Layoff Cooties – It's Them, Not You

I have even read these out loud as I looked at pictures of my former colleagues.

Is that crazy? Maybe. But it is healing. I imagine their responses, apologizing where necessary, and maybe asking me for forgiveness. But I am also cognizant that those are my ideations, not theirs.

I wonder if they think about me as much as I think about them. There are things in my everyday life I still wish to share with them. Something as simple as a family moment, like Ben's graduation from high school, Kelsie making her travel softball team, or some delicious food picture I knew they would salivate over. And then I remember. If they really cared about me, they would reach out.

And so I'm left with these letters, knowing I'm at peace having said everything I wanted to say, even if I couldn't say it to their faces. By writing them down, I no longer have to carry the weight of these feelings.

I vulnerably share them with you in this acceptance chapter and challenge you to do the same writing exercise on your healing journey.

You'll notice that each letter has a distinct tone. I hope you can feel it. Not only in the word choice and pattern of my writing, but in the depths of my heart. This is as vulnerable as I get. I mince no words. These letters are the raw, uncut version. Perhaps by reading mine, you'll feel empowered to write your own. To say all the things you need to say. To find some level of acceptance in responding to those who played a part in your layoff story.

Acceptance—The Gift I Gave Myself

To the real Gordon,

Your true character was revealed to me on November 29, 2023.

Not during my interview process in December 2019.
Not during my first week on the job in February 2020.
And most definitely not during the years when I lined your pockets with nearly five million dollars in software sales as one of your top sales reps and leaders.

No, your true character was hiding behind a black rectangular box on Zoom as you chuckled your way through my four-minute termination speech.

One minute for each year of my service. Is that the formula you use in these situations?

I snapped a photograph of that moment in time. It was 10:46 a.m. (EST) when you joined the call but failed to turn on your video camera to read me my last rites. That physical picture and the one in my mind haunted me for months.

Visceral feelings of anger, disappointment, embarrassment, sadness, and shame.

Each feeling was necessary to be felt on a path toward healing.

No HR representative was on that call.

Just you. My executive sales leader. I use that term loosely because I don't think you were leading anything except for a four-minute session on what not to do.

The disrespect you showed me by not turning on your camera didn't stop me from asking you to turn on yours. Your laugh and cowardly response to the camera not working showed your true character in that very moment.

That picture no longer haunts me.

I look at it today and choose five different words to describe that moment in time: character, courage, strength, transparency, and truth.

I am choosing to focus on MY respectable character, not your disappointing one.

I am choosing to focus on MY unflappable courage, not your embarrassing weakness.

I am choosing to focus on MY unwavering transparency, not your unwillingness to answer my questions.

I am choosing to focus on MY reliable truth, not your scripted corporate narrative.

I don't expect an apology from you. When you blocked me on LinkedIn, you sent a very clear message you wanted to erase me from your network. As if I never existed. As if you could just click a button, and I would disappear forever.

Well, guess what?

I am still here.

I am still standing.

I am still one of the best sales professionals you ever had.

WHAT IF you never read this book? No worries. My true story lives on regardless.

IMAGINE IF your daughters read this book?

If only they knew you were the real Gordon.

When you know better, you do better. Be better, Gordon. If not for me, for them.

— Laura

Acceptance—The Gift I Gave Myself

To the real Bill,

Once upon a time, I thought you were one of the best leaders I ever had.

I trusted you. I believed you. Perhaps that was my first and second mistake.

I thought you would always have my best interests at heart.

Yes, that was my third and final mistake.

It all changed overnight.

The trust was lost forever. And once you lose trust, nothing else really matters.

I think you know what day trust was lost, but just in case you don't remember, it was that fateful day in May when we were all in NYC together for Quarterly Business Reviews. You were upset that I told Kristen about the opportunity for her to move into leadership without you being there. You wanted to deliver the news to her; but I knew better than to let you have that moment surprising her without any notice. I have no regrets in telling her in advance of your big plan while you had Matt believing he was going to get the role instead.

I knew at that moment the chain of events of bullshit corporate politics would begin. Or should I say, continue? The dominoes would fall more quickly and you and Gordon would get what you wanted in the end. Any chance I had to exert authority with my team would be over. Let's face it; any authority I thought I had with my team was under false pretenses during my entire tenure under your reign.

The Layoff Cooties – It's Them, Not You

You and Gordon tried to control my strings like a puppet.

Except I was never one of those corporate marionettes.

I operated without strings.

This separated me from you and the rest of the corporate puppets.

I led completely differently from you. A better way. And everyone knew it.

I led as a servant leader for my people. You led as a corporate politician, giving up your people for your own protection.

Your leadership failed our team when we needed you the most.

Your leadership failed me when I needed you the most.

You retreated, hoping to not be seen. Or heard.

You always said you didn't want to make any waves, so you sat back and let decisions be made for you. That's not leadership.

I lost so much respect for you in the last six months of my tenure when you failed to take action like a real leader does to get answers for his team.

And months after my layoff, when I learned of your own fall from grace and being demoted from leadership to an individual contributor role as a sales rep? I couldn't help but laugh.

I laughed because it's not where you ever wanted to be.

I laughed because the company could have easily demoted me too, but that wasn't my fate.

No, my fate was to record this story. My layoff story. Of which you played a pivotal role.

Acceptance—The Gift I Gave Myself

The role of the corporate politician.
No one is better at playing it than you.

— Laura

To the real Annie,

Congratulations.
    You won. I lost.
    It's unfortunate that has to be the way for so many women in executive positions when surrounded by other strong women in their midst. That we have to feel like one has to lose in order for another to win. Clearly, we still have such a long way to go.
    I thought you were different. I thought wrong.
    But under further review ...
    Here's what you won: a team that fears you.
    When you give directives to our entire Customer Growth team to stop corresponding with me or they would lose their job, that instills a fear-based culture.
    Was that really necessary? I am no threat to you or to them.
    Is that how you want to lead? You're better than that and you know it.
    Here's what I lost: your support and trust. Maybe I never really had it to begin with.
    You won Kristen in the end. The personnel prize you always wanted most.
    The snide comments after she moved to my team never seemed to end.
    You thought they were funny. I did not.

The Layoff Cooties – It's Them, Not You

I often wonder if you regretted introducing me to Kristen back in October 2021.

You always seemed threatened by or jealous of our close relationship.

Don't worry. I lost Kristen in the end. Once I was no longer useful to her career, she disappeared from my life. I can't help but think that makes you happy inside. Again, you won.

You won Bill's adoration. He worshiped you. Everyone saw it and wondered if he could do his job without you in his back pocket. Maybe you enjoyed that position of power?

I lost Bill's trust. And once that happens, there's really no repair, so it was either him or me that had to go.

You won among Gordon's good ole boys club. For dollars and cents, you just dealt with the inequity for years versus standing up for yourself and the women who would follow.

I never wanted to be in that good ole boys club if it meant not being true to who I am.

You won. I lost. It's all about perspective.

It was never a fair game to begin with.

I accept how it all played out.

Win or lose.

— Laura

To the real Kristen,

You broke my heart.

The day you stopped communicating with me was a conscious decision on your part to put our friendship *in a container and seal it. I watched you do this several times with other people when difficult situations arose personally and professionally. I just never thought I would be put in one.*

I did not make up that we had a close friendship. It was real. And it was special. You reminded me of that every day with your heartfelt correspondences. So imagine how I felt when your communication immediately stopped that fateful day.

On November 29th, I lost my job.

On December 5th, I lost my friend.

The latter has been more difficult to grieve and heal. Jobs can be replaced. People cannot.

We partied at a Penn State tailgate, you were a welcomed overnight guest in my home multiple times, and we laughed our way through a rainy, soaking wet Maryland Beer Festival. We planned vacations (that unfortunately never transpired), shared countless charcuterie boards, ate at restaurants you energetically reserved, and promised to take my daughter thrifting in NYC. It was a friendship built on trust, vulnerability, and loyalty.

We sat on countless Zoom calls, supported each other closing many deals, strategized on saving customers at time of their renewal, and fought for respect compared to our colleagues on other sales teams. Our food-and-forecast texts sharing sales updates and plenty of food porn pictures from our diverse meals prepared at home and on our business travels were some of my favorite pings to my phone.

The nearly twenty-year gap in our ages never seemed to matter. There was a mutual respect we built quickly.

The Layoff Cooties – It's Them, Not You

Each of us learned so much. I'll always be grateful for the ripple effect your personal and professional relationship brought to my life.

You are one of the funniest people I've ever met. I think that's what I miss the most. Yes, it's definitely the jokes and the constant laughter.

Don't you miss it too?

You had a special way of influencing my perspective for the better. I wondered, at times, who was mentoring who? I relied on you far too much for that levity during the challenging times. And then, when I needed your friendship the most, you disappeared into thin air.

You had a prolific rise early in your sales career and are no doubt wise beyond your years. You should be very proud of your accomplishments. I'd like to think I had a prominent part in your exponential growth. Based on your caring letters, I know I did.

You still have a lot to learn. You've worked for only two companies in your short, storied career. There's so much MORE for you to experience in the business world versus the toxic, bubbled and fiercely controlled community you work in today.

You've seen the good, the bad, and the ugly up close and personal in corporate America. I pray you never have to experience what I did when standing up for what is morally and ethically right. No one deserves to lose their livelihood AND their friendships because of a layoff.

I can't imagine what it must have been like for you to see your mentor treated disrespectfully, like I was on my last day. In the weeks after my layoff, my good name

Acceptance—The Gift I Gave Myself

was dragged through the mud by people who once put me on a pedestal. Beware of the pedestal. It's not as sturdy as you may think. Anyone can get knocked down. Even the Golden Child. Yes, even you.

You often said my greatest attribute was the confidence and belief I instilled in others.

I believed in you.

I believed in us.

I believed the things you said to me.

I believed the things you wrote to me.

I believed our friendship would last beyond a job, especially when you PROMISED our bond was stronger than work.

But on December 5, 2023, that all changed.

You crushed my beliefs with your silence.

You made me second guess all the things you ever wrote and said to me. You made me wonder if I really was a strong, impactful, and respected leader. You made me rethink my confidence in myself, not only as a decorated colleague, but as a loyal friend.

There were days when I would convince myself she'll reach out today.

But no, nothing. Just silence.

Your silence haunted me for months.

Until ... a shift in my mindset happened one day.

I refused to keep our friendship in your sealed container. It felt trapped and unhealthy inside. Maybe it can exist there for you to deal with later, when you're mature enough to handle the great responsibility our friendship requires. But it couldn't reside there for me to move on, so I opened the container to set those feelings free.

>   Perhaps there are things I'm unaware of that forced your behavior and actions to no longer correspond despite my attempts across multiple channels for months. How you had so much self-control to ignore my countless emails, texts, phone calls, LinkedIn DMs, and snail mail is beyond me. That's not a sign of strength; it's pent-up fear and disassociation to not deal with the hard things in life.
>
>   I believe God brings people into our lives when we need them the most. God also removes them to protect us. I trust He is always in control. You filled that need for two years, and I'm eternally grateful. I hoped our friendship would last a lifetime, but that's not for me to decide.
>
>   God instructs mankind to forgive. As a faithful follower, I can forgive, but I can't forget.
>
>   I forgive your silence, but I can't forget the immense hurt you've caused me.
>
>   I forgive your putting our friendship in a container and sealing it, but I can't forget the unnecessary loss of time trying to understand why.
>
>   For your own healing process, I hope you can open the container again.
>
>   I pray we can be reunited and begin a new friendship because we can't ever go back to the old one.
>
>   No longer heartbroken and container free,
>
>   — Laura
>
> P.S. "An invisible thread connects those who are destined to meet, regardless of time, place, and circumstance. The thread may stretch or tangle. But it will never break." – Ancient Chinese Proverb

Acceptance—The Gift I Gave Myself

The invisible thread quote was special for me and Kristen. We referenced it a lot over the course of our friendship in letters to one another. I include it here again because I want my readers to know that regardless of what happens to us in life, we are shaped by the people who come and go. No one comes to us by accident. Good. Bad. Or indifferent. Each of us plays an important part in each other's life journey.

We are relational beings. God designed us this way. It's part of our DNA. He wants us to build a community with each other.

Find solace in knowing you had an impact on those around you. Tell the people in your life what they mean to you. Write it down. Bring it to life by speaking it out loud. Find ways to let them know. Even when you think it's impossible. There is always a way. When you look at it from that perspective, what's not to accept?

11 From Rejection to Redirection

I was too young to retire officially at age forty-five after my layoff.

My retirement plan was to work in corporate America until I was fifty, and then assess what I wanted to do next. Why do we put these boundaries on milestone years like we are supposed to fit into a nice, neat box? Why I chose fifty, I couldn't tell you, but it seemed like a good round age to reevaluate one's professional career. My layoff sped up those plans by five years.

There's no reason I shouldn't have been able to spend the next five years with the company that laid me off. Even with the PE buyout, there was plenty of opportunity for me to grow and have an impact throughout the organization. I could have moved to an open sales rep role if Gordon didn't want me as a sales leader any longer. He could have placed me in Sales Operations with my years of experience in that area. But no, the corporate lackeys somehow found a spot for Bill to get demoted from leadership and transition to an open sales role with the change of the fiscal year. He had zero proven experience as a sales rep, but the good ole boys club protected him, so there he remains.

I digress.

The Layoff Cooties – It's Them, Not You

As a self-proclaimed workaholic, I love working. Always have. Always will.

In the months after my layoff, we proved we could live off Erik's income alone. I recognize that comes with privilege too. I am married and have a supportive partner with a good-paying job who allows me to take the time I need to figure out what I want to do next. Many folks are not in a stable financial situation when they experience a layoff. They may be single or don't have a supportive partner, either financially or emotionally. They don't have an emergency fund to tap into easily. Their need to find the next paycheck is immediate, which adds to the stressors of losing their job. I feel for everyone in that position, because they are so focused on the financial aspect of finding a job, they rarely have the time to take care of the emotional trauma losing a job creates.

But even with this luxury of not having to worry about my next meal or my mortgage being paid, I wanted to get back to work. Through my strong network, I had folks reaching out shortly after my layoff to see if I was interested in getting back in the game.

That's what it is.

Corporate America is a game, right?

And I had just been played.

I wanted nothing to do with jumping back into the arena where I felt my next sucker punch was awaiting. My working world was different now. The mass layoffs, specifically in tech sales, were not welcoming invitations to lure me back. People I believed had my best interests at heart broke my trust and that fracture was still too fresh. I wasn't interested in starting over at some new company, feeling like

I needed to prove myself all over again. Twenty-five years is a long time to be in sales. I paid my dues. I earned my keep. I did the things I needed to do. I made it. And then they took it away.

Now here I was at age forty-five, feeling like a little kid when someone asks, "What do you want to be when you grow up?"

I wanted to scream: "I have no freaking idea!"

Do any of us know what we want to be when we grow up? Truly.

We think we know what we want, but then when we get there, is it all it's cracked up to be? Usually not. I thought I had my dream job, but look at the nightmarish things that existed long before my layoff. Corporate politics. Pay inequity. Being removed from my former employer's toxic culture forced me to see the cracks in the walls I ignored when I worked there because of my financial success. Golden handcuffs are real, my friends.

For those who have experienced a layoff, I challenge you to remove yourself from the final separation. You no longer work there. What's done is done. But when you worked there, regardless of how short or long your tenure, were you as happy as you thought? Or were there things that made you wonder if that job or company was really the place where you belonged? You now have a clean slate. Just because you spent five, ten, or even twenty-five years like me in one profession, doesn't mean you have to spend the rest of your life there. It's not a prison sentence.

Here's the thing with redirection. There is no right or wrong way to redirect yourself. You have the power to change your mind at any point in the process and redirect yourself to something else if things don't go your way as originally planned.

In sales, reps are always looking for the silver bullet, the secret sauce, the one thing that will magically make their sales turn around. It's never just one thing. It's a culmination of many things. I don't have the answers on your redirection piece, so if you were hoping to find that missing ingredient in these pages, I'm sorry. But I can share my journey with you so far.

The rejection from my former company forced my hand at redirection.

I needed to figure out what was next because I wanted to find meaningful work again. At forty-five years old, I felt like I had another forty-five years to go. We hear so many stories about people finding their passion and purpose in their forties, fifties, sixties and beyond. Why couldn't I be in that mix? Heck, I didn't want to wait another decade; I wanted that passion and purpose immediately.

This is what I knew:

I loved helping people.

I loved leading people.

I loved motivating people.

There are so many professions that fill those three loves.

I decided to give one-on-one sales coaching a try.

In less than three months after my layoff, I formed an LLC and had a website up and running, naming my company Ripple Effect Sales Advisory. I built two sales-based curriculums, one for sales reps called BELIEF and one for first-line sales leaders called TEAMS. I also had monthly options available if folks just wanted to have a sales coach on retainer for ad hoc sales related topics. I wish I could tell you it brought 100 percent satisfaction to my world, but it didn't.

I missed the team aspect. I missed the community. It was difficult for me to see how my impact was helping my clients without being part of their bigger team picture. Even if they felt they got something out of our brief coaching time together, I felt unfulfilled.

My presence on LinkedIn helped attract sales coaching clients, but I noticed myself posting more about stories from my layoff experience than I ever wrote about sales. I commented on many sales influencers' posts, but when defining a niche for myself, I gravitated more toward sharing vulnerable thoughts from my layoff experience. My layoff posts were going viral and resonating with the growing number of people in that community.

One post with the hook line of "Golden handcuffs are real" got nearly 200K views in less than a week. For someone whose normal posts were getting a couple thousand views, this was unprecedented. More and more individual layoff posts started getting 30K, 40K, and 50K views in twenty-four hours or less. My vulnerable storytelling resonated with an unheard community on LinkedIn. My calendar had more meetings from layoff connections than anything sales coaching related. I suppose that was to be expected since I was making a name for myself as someone who vulnerably spoke about my layoff experience.

These viral posts built my confidence. I felt like I was helping people by validating their experiences after a layoff. People wanted to hear from me. They kept coming back for more because they knew I wouldn't sugarcoat the layoff experience. They were there for the emotions. The feelings. The trauma. The grief. The vulnerability. The rejection. And the redirection.

As time went on, I started believing my layoff had happened for a specific reason.

A reason God knew all along was part of me figuring out my purpose in this next phase of life. I wasn't supposed to be in Corporate America anymore. I wasn't supposed to do only sales coaching. It was more than that. I had emerged as a voice for the layoff community. To use my firsthand experience to help others. To speak up for those who are too afraid or not ready to voice their feelings to the world and the ones who are just beginning to find a voice for themselves.

I believe in God-whispers. If you're not familiar with the term, it's an overwhelming sense that you should or shouldn't be doing something coming directly from God. It's like He's whispering in your ear. You must be receptive to hearing it and answering His call. Before I lose all of you nonbelievers out there, feel free to call it "the universe" or whatever name you have for it, but I'm confident you know the feeling I'm talking about. It's innate to us as human beings. For me and my faith, it's a God whisper.

I have this overwhelming feeling that God is telling me, *"Laura, your platform was far too small at your former company. I am preparing you for a much larger platform for you to help people in ways you never imagined."* I believe this with every bone in my body. I have goosebumps when I say it out loud. As I write this book, I am thinking about new ways I can reach the layoff community and how I can build a network, a community that connects people affected by this life-changing event with one another. It would be a place where people feel safe, welcomed, and heard, where they could deal with the emotional trauma losing a job perpetuates. It's part of my redirection story. My timeline. My timing.

No, God's perfect timing.

As an aficionado of personal and professional development, I want to share three exercises that anyone can do to help guide them on their redirection story. In Chapter 9: Testing-Does Anyone Really Know What Works, I call out the elephant in the room. I recognize not everyone can invest in an international retreat to go find the meaning of life on a Mexican mountainside. While there are activities I took part in on that retreat that helped reframe my next chapter in life, I also realized I had many of the answers already myself. I needed a reminder to tap back into them again.

When I look back at my twenty-five-year sales career, everything boiled down to these three things: Attitude, Skill, and Effort. If I was struggling, it was because I didn't have the right attitude (yet). I didn't possess the right skills (yet), or I wasn't putting forth the right effort (yet). I needed to adjust one or more of those three things to make a difference and move the needle. It sounds so simple, but it's true. Everything is Attitude, Skill, and Effort (EASE).

Here are three personal and professional development exercises I share with my sales clients. You don't have to be in sales to complete them. They help you learn more about yourself. I hope you take the time to invest in yourself as part of your redirection story.

Exercise #1

Alphabet Soup

If someone asked you to think of twenty-six things to describe yourself, could you do it? Why twenty-six do you say? Because you have to use a letter of the alphabet to start each description! I'm always looking for new ways to make learning about someone fun and interesting beyond the tell-me-about-yourself question. Before I work with a new sales client, I ask them to complete this Alphabet Soup exercise. This is an opportunity to confirm with yourself, you are who you think you are! And because I don't ask anyone to do anything I wouldn't do myself, here are my answers:

A-Author
B-Ben & Kelsie's Mom
C-Charcuterie Creator
D-Dependable Doer
E-Erik's Wife of 19 Years and Counting
F-Forgiver But Not Forgetter
G-Generous With My Time
H-Hardworking
I-Introverted Individual
J-Jeep Owner
K-Kindhearted Krauss
L-Lego-Loving Laura
M-Mentor & Mentee
N-Nap Taker
O-Open Minded
P-Philanthropic
Q-Quiet Time Finder
R-Restaurant Reviewer
S-Sales Professional
T-Trustworthy
U-Understanding of Differences
V-Vulnerable to a Fault

W-West Islip High School Graduate
X-Xenial (a.k.a. Welcoming ... saving you from googling it)
Y-Youngest of Five Kids
Z-Zero Tolerance for Rude People

Wasn't that fun? Now you try. It's as easy as ABC.

Exercise #2

Your Lifeline and the Story of You
This exercise builds a bit on the first one, but fosters deeper thinking to identify the milestone events that shaped who you are. I did this exercise as part of my first Chief core session and again as part of the Vamonos Experience in Mexico. They varied a bit, but the concept and result are the same. The experiences in our lives shape us. The family that raised us. The educational opportunities we received. The socio-economic environment we thrived or survived. The communities where we lived. And yes, the work experiences we loved and hated.

Draw a line across the middle of a blank piece of paper. At the left end of the line, write your birth date. At the right end of the line, put today's date (don't worry; you're not dead yet, but we need an end point for the exercise)! Above the line and at the top of the page put the word PEAKS and below the line at the bottom of the page, put the word VALLEYS. Write each milestone peak and valley at different heights and depths based on how high or low each life event felt. Identify the year (or years), the people involved, and two or three bullet points to describe how each of those events felt.

Here are a few of my entries, so you get the point:

Peaks:
- Born 1978 – happy childhood, loving home, amazing family
- Graduated high school 1996 – smart, athletic, bright future heading into college
- Early Career 2001-2007 – enjoyable Sales Ops career, loved mentoring
- Married Erik 2005 – new relationship, new house, new baby, new life
- Ben Born 2006/Kelsie Born 2012 – family complete
- SaaS Career 2016-2023 – made lots of money, felt successful, validated

Valleys:
- 1986 – Poppy Died – first experience with family death and loss of grandparent
- 1991 – Nonna Died – regret not saying goodbye to grandmother, bratty teenager
- 1998 – College Depression – couldn't go to class, second-guessing my future
- 2011 – DirectBuy Franchise – bankruptcy, failure, depression, almost died
- 2013 – Dad Alzheimer's Diagnosis – scared, fear of unknown, hard to see decline
- 2019 – Dad Died – mentor is gone, was he proud of me?
- 2023 – Laid Off – disrespected, angry, unfair, lost

Identifying these milestone moments in my life taught me three things:

1. I overcame adversity time and time again.
2. The one constant in both the peaks and valleys was my family.
3. I'm still alive and my line is not over. Whew! There is more life to be lived!

Having completed this exercise at two different points in my life, it also impressed upon me that our feelings about certain milestones change. The events have qualifying significance, but the descriptions after each one sometimes didn't quite pack the same punch. Specifically for the valleys, the longer time elapsed between them, the less those negative feelings felt as insurmountable experiences of grief and loss.

This feeds right into my belief system that grief is not something you get *over*; it is something you get *through*. The grief changes and evolves. I'd be curious to know if having this getting *over* versus getting *through* perspective changes the way you perceive milestone peaks and valleys in your line? It's not for me to know for you, but I guarantee deep in your heart, you know the answer yourself. Maybe not when you first complete the exercise, but later, on your own timeline. Keep drawing that line, my friend. Your story is not over yet and there are more peaks and valleys to be added to your lifeline.

Exercise #3: The Possible Life or Possible Pathways
This final exercise is the one I loved the most from my Vamonos Experience trip to Mexico. Suzanne adapted it from the book by Bill Burnett and Dave Evans called *Designing Your Life: How to Build a Well-Lived, Joyful Life*. This exercise

also builds on the first two but has you imagining three possible future lives for yourself. The key is to make each option as different as possible, while including both personal and professional goals. Consider work, love, health, and play. Here's how it works:

1. Life #1 – What is the life you're living today?
2. Life #2 – What would you do if Life #1 was no longer an option?
3. Life #3 – What would your life look like with no constraints (money, status, age, expectations, etc.)?

The beauty of this exercise is that it forces us to face reality, the life we are currently leading; it opens our minds to a second realistic option for living a different life, with some constraints or things that need changing, but a life achievable to live; and the third option allows us to dream! Having no constraints means anything is possible. Some of you may read into that third option to be unrealistic, but I'd challenge you to think about how old you were when your dreams started fading away?

I don't know about you, but my dreams change and deepen over time. There are things I dreamed about as a little girl that have most definitely come true. Finding my soulmate. Raising a family. Having a pool. (Quick story on that last one: I always wanted an in-ground pool as a kid and my dad told me when I was old enough to pay for one myself, I could get it. Thanks, Dad! I earned enough money when I was Rep of the Year at SAP Concur to fund my pool, so that was my prize. Dream realized in 2018)!

Well, all three childhood dreams came to fruition. Dreams do come true!

We must live in reality, but I hope we never stop dreaming.

My layoff rejection was my reality, but dreams still fill my redirection.

How will you transition from rejection to redirection? Start with a bite of alphabet soup.

12 Finding Your Ripple Effect Again

Grieving my layoff felt like grieving a death. The process was very much the same, which is why I structured this book after the seven stages of grief. I liken the process to when my dad passed away in February 2019 after a long battle with Alzheimer's. The only difference? We could prepare for my dad's passing versus the surprise of my layoff.

We knew my dad's fate.

We practically welcomed it to end his suffering.

We were ready for my dad to leave us in God's perfect timing.

But even knowing his death was going to happen, it still didn't prepare me for how I would handle the grief. None of us knows how we will handle grief until it happens to us. I grieve my father today differently than when he first died. Again, the grief is still there; it evolved. It's not something to get *over*; it's something to get *through*.

My relationship with my dad was very special. I was the last of five kids in a loud, but loving Italian family. My siblings are all eight to twelve years older than me, so I had a very different upbringing than they did. I am the baby of the family. The big joke with my siblings was that my parents didn't plan for me because I was born so much later than the rest of them. I was the "accident," even though they didn't mean it negatively. They were teasing me. As I got older and learned the art and science of procreation, I would reply: "I'm no accident, you are…who plans to have four kids in their first five years of marriage?" I guess that was a slight toward my parents, but it usually shut them all up with a grin.

My dad was a former New York State superintendent of schools. In corporate America lingo, he was the CEO, but for a public school district. He spent over five decades dedicated to serving local school communities on Long Island, balancing budgets, writing grants, and improving public education for thousands of students, teachers, and administrators. State and local government officials sought his counsel to tackle important issues where education was involved. He was a leader in every sense of the word. Many of the leadership lessons I practiced my father's example impressed upon me at an early age. The C-suites from my work tenure didn't cultivate that.

Inspect what you expect.

Embrace being a lifelong learner.

Praise in public, redirect in private.

Ask for what you want without fear.

Everyone has a purpose, regardless of title.

Support your team no matter what factors impact performance.

The list goes on and on.

And if we go back to Chapter 1, you'll recall the lessons of paying it forward and speaking the truth that I learned from my mom. If you're thinking I hit the parental jackpot after reading this book, you're right. I don't take that for granted. You can see how their legacy lives on through me.

I can only hope I honored both my parents with how Ben and Kelsie have been raised. We're all still a legacy in the making and one I'm proud of today.

Looking back at my twenty-five year sales career, I can now see that I upheld all the lessons my mom and dad taught me through their example. The high standards I held for myself in corporate America stemmed from my parents. When destructive behavior reared its ugly head throughout my career, I strived to uphold the lessons they confidently taught me.

I was in junior high when I remember attending a celebration for my dad's retirement in the mid-1990s (the first of many times he "retired"). It was one of those fun-filled evenings where the guest of honor received a lifetime achievement certificate. When it was my dad's opportunity to speak, he respectfully thanked everyone for coming and sharing kind words. But then he did something no one expected.

He took the certificate and folded it in half.

He talked about his early career days and why he chose public education.

He tore the certificate in half.

Without missing a beat, he handed one half to someone in the room.

He folded the remaining half and continued to share stories about his work experiences.

He tore the certificate in half again and handed it to someone else.

He continued this pattern of sharing stories, strolling down memory lane until the entire certificate was no longer in his hands and every piece was now spread throughout the room. He ended by saying his decades of achievements were impossible without everyone else. Big or small, everyone had an important role in the lifetime award the audience perceived as being all his.

Talk about cutting a slice of humble pie and sharing it.

That's who my dad was. He never sought notoriety; he wanted to make a difference.

There was a man at my dad's funeral who introduced himself to my family. He shared how he once was a troubled high school kid in the 1980s and on the brink of being expelled. He had no direction and little support at home. As superintendent, my dad had to meet with him as part of his potential consequences to determine his punishment. He didn't share what my dad said, but he said Dad gave him a second chance. It changed the direction of this man's life because he had never received a second chance before. Over thirty years later, this grown man felt the need to show up at my dad's funeral and share that story with us, complete strangers.

We never know the true ripple effect our daily actions have on others. Sometimes it's immediate when people tell us. Other times, it's more obscure, playing behind the scenes and catapulting a chain of events unknown to us. My dad probably never knew his impact on that man's life who attended his funeral decades later. Maybe he was never supposed to know.

Not having my dad physically present to witness my layoff grief alongside me in person hurt immeasurably. I believe in heaven and knew he was up there watching these events transpire in real time. I talked to my dad all the time, imagining we were sitting at the kitchen table in my childhood home where so many of our father-daughter discussions took place. I thought of things he would say when I pressed him about starting over again at this phase of life.

And then I would just cry.

I cried because I was his baby girl, and I just wanted my dad to hold me in his arms and tell me I was going to be alright.

I cried because even though he was no longer on earth, I still desperately wanted him to be proud of me.

I cried because I had to reinvent myself instead of relying on the stellar reputation I had built for so many years.

I cried because I needed emotional release.

And through the tears, I could feel him wiping them away, one at a time.

I could hear him telling one of his silly dad jokes to make me laugh.

And then I would smile. And laugh. And smile again.

One of my favorite unknown author quotes is: *"Be the things you love most about the people who are gone."* I channeled these feelings about my dad by imagining how he would handle the layoff situation.

What would he want to learn from the experience?

Who would he lean on to help him get through the difficult times?

When would he know when the time was right to move on to the next big thing?

How would he use something bad and turn it into something good, not just for himself, but for others?

I would encourage you to consider these questions regarding your layoff. The answers are not for me to provide in this final chapter of the book. It's your story. Which means it requires your answers. You may even have different questions than the ones I posed.

As I pondered the answers to these questions for myself,

I remembered the eulogy I gave at my dad's funeral. Each of my siblings spoke at the church, and as the baby of the family, I went last. I shared the following memory:

> *There's really only one story I'd like to share with you today in closing. I hope it serves as a capstone for a life well lived. In 2011, my dad and I were sitting alone in my kitchen. He and my mom were visiting my home in Maryland. He had that morning's newspaper in hand as he drank his hot tea. We were just having small talk back and forth when I asked him, "Dad, do you have any regrets in life?"*
>
> *Without hesitation, he folded his newspaper in half and looked me straight in the eye and said, "Laura, your mother and I loved having you five kids. We have ten amazing grandchildren. We traveled the world together, and I was fortunate to have a career that I truly enjoyed. No, I have no regrets."*
>
> *How many of us are lucky enough to say that? And not just say it, but believe it emphatically without hesitation?*
>
> *My dad was not one for long goodbyes. But if there's one thing he always said to me at the end of a phone call, in one of his cards or notes, or simply as I was leaving his house after a visit, it was this ... BE WELL.*

For as prolific a career as my dad had serving others in education over five decades, you'll notice work wasn't the first thing he referenced in my question about his life. He talked about his wife, his kids and grandkids, his travels,

Finding Your Ripple Effect Again

and then work. No regrets about any of them. But work, he listed last.

I'd like to think if someone ever asks me if I have any regrets at the end of my life, my answer would be the same. No regrets. Would I still hold this layoff experience as something that stood in the way of achieving that inner peace? No.

I played the game.

I overcame the shock.

I didn't deny it happened.

I released my anger.

I imagined the strength of my leadership and mentoring impact living on through others.

I told depression it had no place in my life.

I tested multiple coping mechanisms.

I accepted the gift of forgiveness by forgiving others.

I moved from rejection to redirection. Pivoting here and there with more pivots expected.

And I'll continue to find my ripple effect in many waters.

My goals for writing this book were threefold:

1. I wanted to share my personal experience as a top-performing software sales leader blindsided by a targeted and politically motivated layoff.
2. I wanted others to know the raw, visceral feelings of losing a job they loved and the people they worked with are normal. I also wanted them to recognize there is no defined timeline for grieving.
3. I wanted people to learn that rejection from a layoff is simply a redirection to their next big thing in life. They can and will work again!

So, how did I do? Did I meet all three goals? I'm used to crushing my quotas so I hope the answer is a resounding YES!

In the sales world, we'd move the opportunity in Salesforce to Closed-Won or Closed-Lost after the evaluation. I hope I Closed-Won the deal.

This book started out as a healing journey for me, but by the end of the writing process, turned into so much more. You see, this book isn't just for me. It's for you. It's for someone you love. It's even for someone you used to work with as much as you may hate to admit it. Layoff cooties are not make-believe. They are very real. They originated and exist within every organization, so by default, "It's THEM, not YOU." Don't let a decision that was made outside of your control limit how far your ripple effect goes in the world.

This world needs your ripple effect now more than ever.

I used to challenge my sales reps regularly to believe in themselves.

To believe in things greater than they ever imagined.

To believe in their untapped potential.

To break down what seemed like insurmountable goals into bite-sized pieces.

To celebrate the small wins while never losing sight of the bigger picture.

I challenge you to do the same.

I know your layoff seems insurmountable.

I know you have financial stressors.

I know it still hurts emotionally.

But here's what else I know to be true.

Your ripple effect is still being felt at your former company.

The work you did there mattered. The work relationships you fostered mattered more.

YOU MATTER.

I'm asking you to believe in your ripple effect.

You control the new ripples that have yet to make their splash.

They can reach further than you ever imagined.

By reading this book, you are now a part of my ripple effect.

My life is forever changed for the better from my layoff experience.

Your layoff has the power to do the same.

Make a splash, be well, and God bless.

 # Cooties Q & A

If you've experienced a layoff and have the cooties:

1. Few people can forget where they were and what they were doing when they learned of their own layoff. When you think back to that moment in time, what were your first thoughts when you realized your job was gone?

_____

_____

2. We often spend more time at work during the week than we do with our own families. Sometimes the friendships we have with work colleagues can feel just as strong as those close familial relationships. What work relationships have you fostered throughout your career that you would be upset if those friendships suddenly disappeared?

_____

_____

3. Our jobs and careers can feel like the main part of our identity. When we lose a job through no fault of our own, like with a layoff, there can be a loss of self. Do you identify yourself with your career and what can you do to remind yourself that you are so much more than your job?

_____

_____

_____

4. Most people focus on the financial aspects of a layoff as being the most stressful part of transitioning to their next role. Aside from the financial impact, what part of the emotional side of a layoff has been the most difficult for you to cope with as part of your healing journey?

_____

_____

_____

If someone you love has the cooties:

1. Seeing people we love go through difficult times is hard to watch. What was your initial reaction when you learned that your loved one lost their job, and do you think you would say or do anything differently?

   _____

   _____

2. Spouses play an important role in the support of their partners. If your spouse and/or partner was laid off, how did that life-changing event impact the dynamics of your family and your relationship?

   _____

   _____

3. Knowing what to say (and what not to say) to a loved one experiencing a layoff can feel like walking on eggshells! How can you be a beacon of hope and support to your loved one?

   _____

   _____

The Layoff Cooties – It's Them, Not You

4. Kids are observant and know when something is wrong, despite our best efforts to shield them from life changes like a layoff. How do you think families should discuss layoffs in an age-appropriate way?

_____

_____

If you're the one left behind at work and afraid to get the cooties:

1. Companies resort to layoffs for many reasons. When your colleagues leave the organization because of a layoff, how do you feel about the company you still work for and for those let go?

_____

_____

2. Survivor guilt is a response to an event in which someone else experiences loss, but you did not. How does your colleague's layoff impact your own roles and responsibilities and is there a part of you that feels any sense of survivor's guilt?

_____

_____

3. Think of at least three people you know your company laid off. What can you do TODAY to let each of them know you're there to support them?

___

___

4. Sometimes saying nothing at all sends just as strong a message as fearing you'll say the wrong thing. Does the adage, "out of sight, out of mind" apply to your experience when you lose touch with colleagues your company lays off, or are there other reasons you choose to no longer communicate with them?

___

___

 # Acknowledgments

There are so many people to thank for their support of this passion project of mine. Each played a special part during the process, so why not show my gratitude with a little Alphabet Soup?

Let's have some fun.

A is for Ally Berthiaume. Part writing coach, part therapist, as I like to describe you. I don't know if you fully grasp just how AMAZING you are at what you do, but I can't imagine this authoring journey without you. I knew within the first few minutes of meeting you that you were the one! By living out your bravery, you instill belief in your clients to live out theirs. Not only was this writing journey a cathartic one, you made it a positive overall experience. I cannot recommend you enough to future authors. Keep being you, my friend. There is no one better!

B is for my son Ben. I am so proud of the young man you have become. I cried when I found out I was pregnant with you. I did so because I was scared, and didn't think I was ready to be a mom. You taught me everything I needed to

The Layoff Cooties – It's Them, Not You

know one day at a time, and guess what? I'm still learning from you (and Kelsie) all these years later. Love you, BUBS.

C is for corporate America. You may laugh at this one, but I'm extremely grateful for all the lessons learned over nearly twenty-five years in that arena. It's an environment like no other, and I took advantage of every opportunity to hone my leadership skills from a very early age. It takes COURAGE to stand up for what's right in corporate America. No regrets.

D is for Diane Higgenbothem. Thank you for answering my call on November 29, 2023. Actually, thank you for answering all my calls when I need to be reminded of God's DIVINE grace. You have no idea what your specific prayer meant for me on that fateful day. God knew it was just what I needed. Thank you for your friendship and your delicious strawberry cake.

E is for my husband Erik. You never cease to amaze me how you support EVERYTHING we face together with a genuine respect for one other. We've had quite the roller coaster ride in the last twenty-five years together. Buckle up as the best is yet to come. I don't make it easy, but thank you for loving me. You are my soulmate, now and forever. Love you so much.

F is for my Frederick Christian Fellowship (FCF) Church peeps. From my Wednesday night Bible study group to my charcuterie-eating IF Real Table women's group to my inaugural Financial Peace University (FPU) small growth group,

Acknowledgments

your FAITHFUL support long before this book writing journey started will hold a special place in my heart always.

G is for God. Thank you for creating me and loving me no matter what. You know my purpose and what You placed me on earth to do. I know if I follow your Word, I can't go wrong.

H is for Hope. I am thankful for the hope each new day brings. HALLELUJAH!

I is for my in-laws, Craig and Kathy Krauss and my brother-in-law Ryan and his family (Sara, Ella, and Morgan). Thank you for welcoming me into the Krauss clan long before Erik and I made it official all those years ago. Here's to many more ICE CREAM visits at Hoffman's in the years to come. Because there's always room for Hoffman's, right?

J is for Judy Howard Ellis. There's a reason why I listened to Ally's "Open Book Broadcast" that particular day. It's where I was first introduced to you and your editorial services at Daybreak Lit. No JOKING … thank you for your help with all the line editing along the way.

K is for my daughter Kelsie. You completed our family tree and blossomed into a beautiful and confident young lady. I'm most proud of your KIND heart, your genuine care for others, and your help dressing me somewhat fashionably with your trendsetting ways. Your future's so bright; keep shining. Love you, Kels.

The Layoff Cooties – It's Them, Not You

L is for the LinkedIn Community. I would double the word count of this book, listing every single one of you who affected my LIFE in those early days of finding my voice after my layoff. Social media was not my forte, but you showed up for me in ways that made me a new believer in the platform's power. I dedicate this book to you because you were there when I needed to connect the most. Again, you know who you are, and I thank you from the bottom of my heart.

M is for Me. Yes, I'm thanking myself. This book is a culmination of forty-five years (so far) of my life. The chapters of this book began when God envisioned me and my story continues to be written all these years later. Congratulations, Laura. You are exactly where you're MEANT to be.

N is for my New York roots. I'm thankful for the first eighteen years of my life living on the South Shore of Long Island with my big, Italian family. I knew all four of my grandparents, played with many of my cousins, and grew up in a household where love was always NEAR. I learned to use my voice early (not only to get some of my mom's mashed potatoes before my siblings finished them all, but to speak up for myself in more serious situations). Well, those mashed potatoes are pretty good, so I consider that a serious situation!

O is for Outliers. The Outlier Project (TOP) led by our fearless leader, Scott MacGregor, lives up to every expectation of the mantra, People Over Everything. Scott, you've created a wonderful community of OUTSTANDING individuals leading extraordinary lives. Thank you for welcoming me into your supportive group with introductions to hundreds

Acknowledgments

of fellow Outliers who are taking advantage of our only one life mindset. #Only1Life

P is for the Pecorale clan. My first immediate family, composed of my parents, Tony (in heaven) and Maria, and my four older siblings, Anthony, Erica, Ralph, and Paul. Jen, Mark, Francesca, Diane, and Nadia would join in the fun later. Nieces and nephews would soon follow: Hillary, AJ, Luca, Aidan, Michael, Evan, Giancarlo, and Saige. Decades have passed us by but make no mistake, your impact on who I've become is PARAMOUNT to every experience I've had personally and professionally. Love you all. Be well.

Q is for the Quitters. Thank you to everyone who QUIT that negative self-talk that falsely said you're not worthy after your layoff. You don't have the layoff cooties. It's them, not you.

R is for the Readers. This book may have started out as my healing journey, but my faith tells me it never was intended for me alone. My story is your story. And our collective story is part of His story. REMEMBER, we are all connected by the power of our stories.

S is for Sales. What an epic career the sales profession has afforded me over the years! Thank you to my prospects, customers, work colleagues, and leaders (the good, the bad, and the ugly). While I'm SADDENED our time ended, it sure was a lot of fun over the years. I won't forget you; I ask you to do the same for me.

T is for Toni Serofin. This beautiful book cover design and formatting reflect your decades of experience in this space. I knew your keen eye for detail and TIMELESS recommendations would make this book look its best. Thank you for all your hard work, advice, and education along the way!

U is for the Unknowns. Thank you to the unknown variables in life that keep me guessing and not being too complacent in the status quo. There may be unknowns, but this layoff experience proved I don't fear the unknown anymore. This I UNDERSTAND.

V is for Vamonos Executive Coaching founded by Suzanne Roske. Thank you for creating a VOCATIONAL retreat for me and our inaugural group of women to your special place in Oaxaca, Mexico. It was a trip of a lifetime, and I'm so grateful to have participated! Hey, I may even be a regular hiker now. Umm … probably not.

W is for my Willing Warriors (aka Beta and Advanced Readers). Dennis Geelen, Dan Goodman, Leslie Wierich, and Mike Antonello—your initial Beta Reader feedback, recommendations, and overall support confirmed what I was sharing would impact others. My Advanced Readers, thank you for your words of praise: Robynn Storey, Scott MacGregor, Suzanne Roske, Renee Devore Wright, Heather Bell, Deborah Brown-Volkman, Erin Harrigan, Sarah Manley, Diane Higgenbothem, Heidi Solomon-Orlick, Dr. John Page, and Beth Stowell Reed.

Acknowledgments

X is for my Xenial college girlfriends. Erin Hoyle, Alison Raynor-Smith, Kara Sasse, and Emily Scott: from College Avenue to Red Lane, Cape Charles, Richmond, Charleston and all the laughs in between, thank you for your friendship and smiles all these years. Yeah, I think sixty gummies is a perfect amount for the long weekend.

Y is for You. Thank you for your time and investment reading my layoff story. I pray you learned something about YOURSELF along the way.

Z is for Zoom. Over 400 and counting of you met with me via Zoom calls in the weeks and months after my layoff and during the writing of this book. And while I can't wait to meet some of you In Real Life (IRL), for now, Zoom will have to do!

About the Author

Laura Krauss is an accomplished sales professional who spent the last twenty-five years honing her sales and leadership skills in the hospitality, pharmaceutical, medical publishing, and software sales industries. After a shocking layoff in the tech space where she was a consistent top-performing sales rep and leader, Laura founded Ripple Effect Sales Advisory LLC where she provides individual virtual sales coaching for quota carrying reps and first-time sales leaders.

Visit her sales coaching website **www.rippleeffectsales.com** for more information on services she offers. She can be reached at **laura@rippleeffectsales.com**.

Besides one-on-one sales coaching, she expanded her leadership skills by creating and hosting an online membership community called "The Layoff Cooties Couch." It's the safest seat to connect with others healing from the emotional trauma of a layoff. The community is all about encouragement and support; and healing through sharing the collective stories with one another. There is also access to coaching and counseling events as well as resources for those experiencing the stages of grief from a layoff.

Laura lives in Maryland with her husband Erik and their two children, Ben and Kelsie. In her spare time, she loves reading, creating delicious charcuterie boards to enjoy with family and friends, and having fun with her side hustle of rebuilding unfinished LEGO sets to resell on eBay.

Laura posts daily on LinkedIn on various topics related to layoffs and life. You can find more information on 'The Layoff Cooties Couch' community on her LinkedIn Featured Section. She loves interacting with her growing social platforms and welcomes the opportunity to connect!

Please follow or connect with Laura here: **https://www.linkedin.com/in/laura-krauss-sales-advisory/**

www.ingramcontent.com/pod-product-compliance
Lightning Source LLC
LaVergne TN
LVHW051219300125
802500LV00004B/25